Strategic Planning Workbook
Revised and Updated

Strategic Planning Workbook
for Nonprofit Organizations

Revised and Updated

Bryan W. Barry

AMHERST H.
WILDER
FOUNDATION

SAINT PAUL,
MINNESOTA

This book was developed by the Services to Organizations'
Community Services Group, a program of the Amherst H.
Wilder Foundation in Saint Paul, Minnesota. The Community
Services Group works in the Twin Cities metropolitan area
and nationally to strengthen the capacity of individuals,
organizations, and other groups to improve their communities.

The Amherst H. Wilder Foundation is one of the largest and
oldest endowed human service and community development
organizations in America. For more than ninety years, the
Wilder Foundation has been providing health and human
services that help children and families grow strong, the
elderly age with dignity, and the community grow in its
ability to meet its own needs.

We hope you find this book helpful! Should you need
additional information about our services, please contact:
Community Services Group, Amherst H. Wilder Foundation,
919 Lafond Avenue, Saint Paul, MN 55104, (651) 642-4022.

For information about other Wilder Foundation publications,
please see the back of the book or contact: Publishing Center,
Amherst H. Wilder Foundation, 919 Lafond Avenue, Saint
Paul, MN 55104, 1-800-274-6024, www.wilder.org

Edited by Vincent Hyman
Illustrated by Patrice Barton
Designed by Rebecca Andrews

Manufactured in the United States of America

Third printing, February 2001

Library of Congress Cataloging-in-Publication Data

Barry, Bryan W.
    Strategic planning workbook for nonprofit organizations / by Bryan
W. Barry. -- Rev. and updated.
        p.   cm.
        ISBN 0-940069-07-5
        1. Nonprofit organizations--Planning.   2. Strategic planning.
    I. Amherst H. Wilder Foundation.   II. Title.
    HD62.6.B37   1997
    658.4'012--dc21
                                        97-8103
                                        CIP

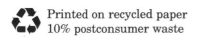
Printed on recycled paper
10% postconsumer waste

About the Author

Bryan W. Barry is director of Services to Organizations for the Amherst H. Wilder Foundation. Each year, his division provides consultation and other assistance to more than five hundred nonprofit, governmental, and community organizations, and provides training for more than eight thousand leaders.

Mr. Barry has consulted on strategic planning and other topics with nonprofits, businesses, government agencies, and community groups across the country. He speaks frequently on issues related to nonprofit management and community development.

Mr. Barry holds a master of arts degree in organizational behavior from the University of Minnesota and a master of divinity degree from Luther Theological Seminary.

Acknowledgments

Each day I learn things that help me in this work—from my colleagues at Wilder, the people and organizations we team up with, colleagues around the country, things people send me to read, and family and friends. I am thankful for you all. Trying to name the individuals who have contributed seems too big a task for this workbook, so I'll not start.

I thank First Banks for their funding of the development costs of the original workbook. I also thank the leadership of North End Area Revitalization (N.E.A.R.), International Youth Foundation, Luther Theological Seminary, Metro Deaf Senior Citizens, Model Cities Inc., and Neighborhood Development Center for allowing us to use examples from their organizations' strategic planning.

Throughout the book I sometimes use the word "we" in making a suggestion about strategic planning or in noting something we at the Wilder Foundation have learned through our work over the years. I am especially indebted to and appreciative of my colleagues at Wilder for what they've taught me. Much of what you find useful in this workbook probably comes from back-and-forth discussions with them. The "we" is intended to acknowledge that fact. However, please note that there is considerable variety in how our staff approach strategic planning and help organizations do it. The shortcomings of this book should be attributed to me and not to them.

Again, thanks to you all.

Bryan Barry
April, 1997

Contents

Section I   Introduction to Strategic Planning

Section II   Developing Your Strategic Plan

A step-by-step approach including worksheets and planning tips.

Section III Appendices and References

Section IV Worksheets

Foreword

In 1986 the Wilder Foundation produced the first edition of this *Strategic Planning Workbook*. Our goal with the original workbook was to produce an easy-to-use primer for nonprofit organizations on strategic planning. Since that time we have received many helpful comments and suggestions from people who have used the workbook. Our staff have also learned and tested new ways to assist nonprofit organizations, community groups, government, broad-based coalitions, and wider movements with their planning. Most of Wilder's consulting staff, including myself, now approach strategic planning somewhat differently than described in the 1986 edition of this book.

In this second edition, we have tried to maintain the primer-like quality of the workbook, and also to incorporate a number of the helpful lessons and suggestions from Wilder Foundation staff, from many nonprofit leaders and consultants, and from our experience since the first edition was published. Substantive changes include:

- Using a steering group to guide the planning so that a wider range of people and groups can contribute.

- Changes in suggested ways to "take stock" of your organization's situation and to develop a shared vision for your nonprofit's future.

- Addition of a fourth method for setting the future direction of your organization—the alignment approach—in Step 3 of the planning.

- More information on common strategies used by nonprofit organizations to address the opportunities and challenges we and the nonprofit sector now face.

- New suggestions on the format of strategic plans.

- A new, more detailed sample strategic plan.

- Additional tips for successfully implementing and updating your strategic plan.
- Material on how multiple organizations, coalitions, and communities can use strategic planning.

We continue to ask for your suggestions about this workbook—what you find useful, where the book is not helpful, and what you are learning about strategic planning that might help other organizations. We hope that such planning will increasingly become an effective tool for nonprofit organizations and broader coalitions to clarify their goals and mobilize the resources required to improve our communities and society.

Introduction to Strategic Planning

In the early 1980s growing numbers of nonprofit organizations began to develop strategic plans. Many nonprofits have found such planning to be a key to their success. Others have not had such a good experience with planning. They got bogged down in the process, or developed a strategic plan that was not particularly useful.

This workbook will introduce you to an approach to strategic planning that has been used by nonprofit groups across the U.S. and in many other countries. The workbook is a step-by-step guide for developing and implementing a useful strategic plan.

Over the past fifteen years, Wilder Foundation consulting staff have received several thousand consulting and training requests from many kinds of nonprofit and government groups—citizen groups, community-based organizations, national and international nonprofits, foundations, government at all levels, and broad-based coalitions or movements dedicated to particular goals. Each year, the most frequent request we receive is for help with strategic planning. Such requests might begin:

- "With the funding cuts we face, our financial situation looks very tight this year and horrible after that."

- "The rules seem to be changing. Funders want to see measurable outcomes. The competition for support is stiffer. Collaborations are being pushed. Organizations are merging. We need to sort through these things and develop a clear plan for the future."

- "Our city is rapidly changing. Despite the best efforts of our organization and many others, things are not improving."

- "Over the past few months, people have approached us with ten new program opportunities. We need to decide which ones to pursue, and how much growth we can handle."

- "We're being criticized for losing our focus and not being responsive to urban neighborhoods."

- "We are about to begin the search for a new executive director, and need to be clearer about our future direction in order to pick the right person."

- "The last time our organization tried to do strategic planning, it was a nightmare."

- "My board chair is encouraging us to develop a strategic plan. To be honest, with all the things on our plate, I don't know if we can handle this now."

. . . or simply . . .

- "We need a strategic plan, but are not sure how to proceed."

- "It's time to update the strategic plan we developed last year."

These comments point to good reasons to develop a strategic plan. Rapidly changing community conditions often require new responses and alliances. A desire to have greater impact leads others to plan. New financial pressures or competition sometimes forces an organization to plan for its very survival. For still other nonprofits, strategic planning is a good way to align their mission, programs, resources, and relationships. Increasingly, funders and regulators ask that the groups they support have some kind of plan for the future.

Even though interest in strategic planning is widespread, significant numbers of nonprofits have had some difficulty with it—particularly the first time through. There was confusion about how to plan, the process did not fit, key people were not productively engaged, the facilitation was poor, the planning was undertaken at a bad time, or some approach other than strategic planning would have been more appropriate at the time. All of these problems can be avoided with a little forethought and preparation.

This workbook is a step-by-step guide for developing a strategic plan for a nonprofit organization, unit of government, community group, or coalition. We have found that the book is useful as:

- A general introduction to strategic planning

- A guide for a nonprofit to develop a strategic plan

- A tool for consultants, trainers, organizers, or volunteers who assist nonprofit groups with such planning

The workbook is divided into four main sections. Section I is an overview of strategic planning that describes:

- What strategic planning is
- Why you should do it—and what its limitations are
- How you can develop a strategic plan in a way that fits your organization

Section II of the book is a step-by-step guide for developing, implementing, and updating a strategic plan. Section III includes tips for planning with multiple organizations and communities, an example of one organization's strategic plan, endnotes, and a bibliography. Section IV contains blank worksheets which you can use in your planning.

What Is Strategic Planning?

Strategic planning is the process of determining: (1) **what** your organization intends to accomplish, and (2) **how** you will direct the organization and its resources toward accomplishing these goals over the coming months and years (see Figure 1). Such planning usually involves fundamental choices about:

- The mission, goals, or vision your organization will pursue
- Whom you will serve
- The organization's role in the community
- The kinds of programming, services, or products you will offer
- The resources needed to succeed—people, money, expertise, relationships, facilities, and so forth
- How you can best combine these resources, programming, and relationships to accomplish your organization's mission

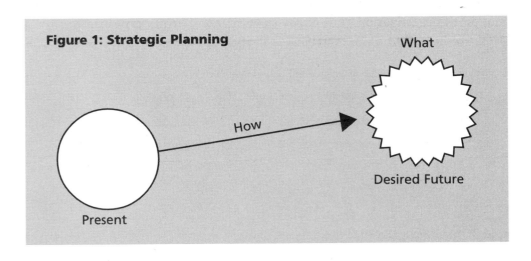

Figure 1: Strategic Planning

What

How

Desired Future

Present

Strategic planning is often distinguished from another kind of planning—*operational* or *short-range planning*. Operational planning is what non-profit organizations do when they develop yearly work plans and budgets. Operational plans are usually more narrow in scope than strategic plans and focus on a shorter period—for example, one year instead of three or five. Both kinds of planning are useful. Strategic planning can be used to chart the longer-term direction and goals for your organization. Operational plans can then be developed to show how, in the coming year, your organization will move toward the future described in its strategic plan.

We are often asked, "How many years should a strategic plan cover?" As a guideline we suggest that you consider a period long enough to make major shifts in your organization's direction, but not so long as to seem absurd. Generally, small nonprofits that operate in quickly changing environments plan two to three years into the future. A three- to ten-year perspective is more common for larger organizations, which may require a longer lead time to make major changes.

Although this workbook focuses on strategic planning for a nonprofit organization, such planning can also be used as an effective tool by divisions or programs within an organization, by coalitions or initiatives involving a number of organizations, or by entire neighborhoods or communities. Appendix A, Planning with Multiple Organizations and Communities, on pages 79-85 discusses these uses of strategic planning. First we will focus on planning for a single nonprofit organization.

Developing a Vision

Stated another way, strategic planning is developing a shared vision of your nonprofit's future, then determining the best way to make this vision occur. By "vision" we mean a shared picture of the future you seek to create—what you believe the organization can accomplish. As people within your nonprofit create a clear and compelling picture of the organization's future, they become committed to helping that future occur. A clear sense of purpose and direction also guides staff in making everyday choices about which opportunities they will pursue, and which they will not.

Strategic planning is also charting a course that you believe is wise, then adjusting that course as you gain more information and experience. The vast majority of nonprofit organizations we serve get better at their planning over time. You cannot develop a perfect strategic plan; the world changes too quickly. Most organizations use their strategic planning to get general agreement on where the organization should be headed, along with the major steps or paths to get there. The plan serves as an orienting vision which helps people and programs keep moving toward agreed-upon goals. As people learn which strategies work (and which do not) and where the most fruitful opportunities lie, they adjust their goals and path accordingly. With experience, their planning and execution improve. Henry Mintzberg, noted professor of management at McGill University, states that strategic planning is like molding a clay pot over time. The design gets clearer and better after you begin shaping your organization's future and determining what's possible. Therefore, many organizations formally update their strategic plan regularly (every one to three years) and make more frequent adjustments in strategy as they learn what works.

Finding the Fit

How does an organization determine the best course for the future? One key is to *find the fit* among three forces—your organization's mission, outside opportunities, and your organization's capabilities:

- The mission of your organization—what you intend to accomplish, your organization's overall goal, the reason you exist.

- Opportunities or threats your organization faces—related to the resources and needs of the people you serve, other stakeholders, competitors and allies, or other major forces (social, economic, political, or technological) that will influence whether you succeed or fail.

- Your organization's capabilities—the resources or competence that your nonprofit has or could develop.

Figure 2 depicts the fit among these forces.

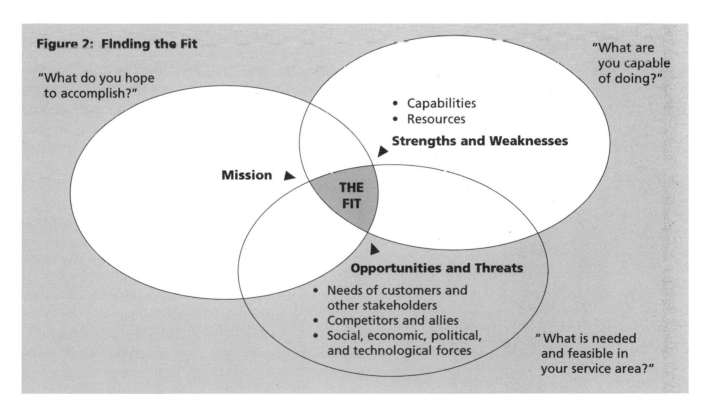

Figure 2: Finding the Fit

"What do you hope to accomplish?"

"What are you capable of doing?"

- Capabilities
- Resources

Strengths and Weaknesses

Mission ▶

THE FIT

Opportunities and Threats

- Needs of customers and other stakeholders
- Competitors and allies
- Social, economic, political, and technological forces

"What is needed and feasible in your service area?"

If there is not sufficient overlap or fit between your organization's mission, its capabilities, and the needs and opportunities of your service area, then your nonprofit is in jeopardy. For example, assume that your mission is to improve the availability and quality of affordable housing across a particular section of town, but you have been unable to convince funders, lenders, and several key community groups to provide significant support to your work. In addition, you do not yet have the capability to undertake housing improvement efforts on the scale you would like.

In this example, your organization has not yet found a good fit between your mission, your capabilities, and the opportunities in your neighborhood. Your strategic planning should help you understand what is occurring, then develop a better approach for the future. The planning will help you answer such questions as: "Is our mission still on target? Why are funders and other community groups not supporting us as we would like? How can additional support be secured? How ambitious should our production goals be (for rehabilitation, new construction, improvement loans)? How will we develop the necessary capabilities to achieve these goals?" When completed, your strategic plan will describe what your organization intends to accomplish over the next few years, the planned scope of that work, and how you will build or secure the resources and support needed to successfully carry out those plans. If you have done good planning, your organization's mission, its capabilities, and external forces and opportunities will be much better aligned.

In summary, strategic planning is the process of developing a shared vision of your organization's future, and the major steps you will take to move the organization in that direction. Such planning will help an organization find the best fit between its mission, its capabilities, and its opportunities.

Why Develop a Strategic Plan—and the Limitations of Formal Planning

Potential Benefits . . .

Why should a nonprofit organization develop a plan for the future?

Improved results

Studies have consistently shown that vision, planning, and goal setting can positively influence organizational performance. Great leaders and great movements have shown that compelling visions have power to draw people toward that future. Studies also show that both large and small businesses which have strategic plans outperform their counterparts without formal plans. Having a clear plan for the future and periodically monitoring progress can also contribute to a greater sense of purpose, movement, and accountability.

Momentum and focus

Leaders of some nonprofit organizations have become so preoccupied with day-to-day pressures that their organizations lose all sense of mission, momentum, and direction. Good strategic planning forces future thinking and can build commitment to agreed-upon goals. It can refocus and reenergize a wandering organization.

Problem solving

Productive planning focuses on an organization's most critical problems, choices, and opportunities. Nonprofit organizations sometimes face a web of problems and opportunities which are hard to address one by one. Strategic planning is a way to resolve an interrelated set of issues or problems in an intentional, coordinated manner. For example, the 1980s and 1990s brought funding cuts, increased competition, and other new demands for many nonprofits. Faced with a severe financial squeeze, organizations have used strategic planning to sort through options such as finding new ways to increase revenue, making choices about service priorities, finding ways to cut expenses, forming mergers or alliances, influencing policy makers, or even calling it quits.

Teamwork, learning, and commitment

Most nonprofits involve people throughout the organization—and often beyond—in developing their strategic plan, such as board members, staff, consumers of service, and organizational allies. Strategic planning provides an excellent opportunity to build a sense of teamwork, to promote learning, and to build commitment across the organization and with key publics. For example, in discussing an organization's history, current situation, and future options, people learn from the ideas and perspectives contributed by others. Participants often come to understand more clearly how their own work meshes with that of others. The planning can also be a way for leaders and work groups to model new behavior. As a clear direction develops for the organization, people usually become committed to this direction if they have contributed significantly in forming it and can connect with it personally. A stronger sense of teamwork and contribution often results from successfully implementing a strategic plan.

Communication and marketing

A good strategic plan can be an effective communication and marketing tool. Board members, staff, funders, and other stakeholders are usually quite interested in where the organization is headed and how their contribution will fit. Increasingly, funders and regulators ask that an organization have a strategic plan in place as a condition of continued support.

Greater influence

With today's pressures, the executives and boards of nonprofits sometimes feel less like "shakers and movers" and more like "the shaken and the moved." Strategic planning can help an organization provide greater influence over its circumstances and world, rather than simply responding to an unending series of problems.

A natural way to do business

Strategic planning has become a natural part of doing business for many organizations. They chart their long-term course, develop yearly plans to implement this direction, take action, monitor progress, and adjust plans and actions based on changing conditions. Planning becomes a familiar part of moving the organization forward and increasing its effectiveness.

. . . and Limitations

Traditional strategic planning also has its limitations.

Costs can outweigh benefits

Strategic planning can consume time and money which might be spent more productively on other tasks. In addition, planning efforts sometimes get off track: Bad decisions are made, smoldering problems surface, people can become lost in the planning process or get bogged down in trivia. Before undertaking a planning effort, you need to ask, "As we imagine how the planning will proceed, does it seem like the benefits of such planning outweigh the costs?" If the answer is no (that is, if costs appear to outweigh the benefits), we suggest that you reconsider whether it is wise to proceed with your planning in this manner. You may need to address a pressing problem, develop a better approach to the planning, or get advice before you begin.

When poor plans are likely

Critics of strategic planning note that some organizations develop lousy plans. Faulty assumptions about the future, poor assessment of an organization's capabilities, poor group dynamics, and information overload are four reasons often cited. If you believe that your planning is or will be unproductive, we suggest you raise the issue early, then correct the problem or get help before proceeding. One technique for reducing the risk of bad decisions is to be clear about the conditions under which you will undertake any major change. For example, "We will not begin program X until Y is in place." A second technique is to build in regular progress reviews and to update the plan regularly. This is especially important when there is a great deal of risk in your strategic plan.

Intuition and creative muddling are sometimes superior to traditional planning

Some organizations are fortunate to have gifted leaders with finely developed intuition about what will occur and how their organizations should proceed. In one sense, strategic planning can be viewed as an effort to duplicate what goes on in the mind of a gifted intuitive leader. Such people know well the strengths and weaknesses of their organizations; they often see opportunities and threats before others do; they know instinctively the best way to proceed—sometimes without formal planning. Albert Einstein wrote:

> I believe in intuition and inspiration . . . at times I feel certain that I am right while not knowing the reason. . . . Imagination is more important than knowledge. For knowledge is limited, whereas imagination embraces the entire world, stimulating progress, giving birth to evolution.

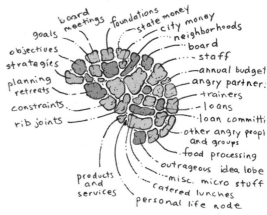

What goes on in the mind of a gifted, intuitive leader *

* Our thanks to Joe Errigo, executive director of Common Bond Housing Corporation in St. Paul, for this illustration of Neighborhood Development Center president Mike Temali's brain.

If your organization has such a leader or leaders, make sure they have ample opportunity to contribute their vision, leadership, and insight throughout the planning. You may want to keep the planning very simple.

Other organizations have developed an operating style which could be called "creative muddling." In its best form, creative muddling occurs when a skilled team of people—who know each other's talents and abilities— work together creatively and opportunistically to achieve a particular purpose or goal. If you have ever watched a really good jazz group, a good "run-and-gun" basketball team, or a skilled kayaker in a fast-moving river—that's creative muddling. Done well, this can be a very effective form of operating. Done poorly, a muddling style can bog down an organization. If such a style really works for your organization, you may want to avoid a strategic planning approach that is laborious or complicated. Such organizations often use a quick-moving strategic planning process which clarifies ultimate goals or a vision of organizational success. Then staff are encouraged to work together creatively to achieve those ends, within some general guidelines and structure.

When critical problems should be addressed first

Organizations in crisis should generally consider tackling immediate, life-threatening problems before proceeding with strategic planning. For example, an organization with severe cash shortages may need to improve its cash situation to workable levels before developing a strategic plan. Hiring a new executive director, when an organization has been without one for some time, may also be a more important task. Organizations customarily need some stability in order to get through a strategic planning process or make very good use of such planning.

When implementation is unlikely

Many of us have had the experience of pouring our energy and ideas into a project that was never implemented. Disillusionment, cynicism, and feelings of powerlessness often result. If leaders have little intention of following through on plans, it may be wiser not to ask staff and board to invest their time and energy in such planning. You save time and bruised expectations. Good plans need good implementation.

The cautions outlined above are not meant to discourage or deter you from developing plans for the future. Strategic planning can be a powerful and practical tool to clarify and achieve your organization's mission. Rather, we are suggesting that you proceed wisely with your strategic planning. Time invested at the front end of the process to anticipate problems and design a workable planning process usually results in much smoother and more effective planning as you proceed.

How to Develop a Strategic Plan

Each nonprofit organization has a distinctive situation and style. Research and our own experience strongly suggest that you use a strategic planning process that fits your organization and context. Nonprofits sometimes run into problems when they try to duplicate the planning process used by an organization that operates in a very different field, sector, or situation.

Over the years, the Wilder Foundation has developed and refined a flexible five-step model to guide nonprofit organizations in developing their strategic plans (see Figure 3). These five basic steps can be adapted to fit the needs, situation, and style of your organization. We encourage you to adapt your strategic planning to fit such factors as your experience with planning, the issues you face, the size of your organization, the time available, leadership considerations, and the number of people and groups to be involved. Our consultants vary their approach to strategic planning around these and other considerations.

Our basic strategic planning process is briefly summarized below and in Figure 3, with each step described in more detail in Section II of the workbook. Practical suggestions for shaping a planning process to fit your organization are also noted below.

Step 1: Get Organized

Your first step is to organize the planning process. This step usually includes deciding that strategic planning is appropriate at this time; selecting a person or steering group to keep the planning on track; determining what people and groups will be involved; deciding if you need a consultant or other resource people; outlining the planning steps; and getting agreement to proceed. Pages 24-35 contain a number of suggestions for getting your planning process organized and off to a good start.

Step 2: Take Stock (Situation Analysis)

In Step 2, organizations often review their history and current situation, then begin to identify future possibilities and choices. From this analysis you will identify the most critical issues or choices concerning your organization's future. Several ways to "take stock" and identify key strategic choices are outlined on pages 36-51.

Step 3: Set Direction

In Step 3, leaders determine the best future direction for the organization, then develop a first draft of the strategic plan. That draft customarily includes the organization's future mission, a vision or overall approach for accomplishing this mission, and specific goals or strategies for moving the organization in the direction envisioned. Some strategic plans also include more detailed information related to future services, finances, staffing, other key issues, and implementation. Alternative ways to determine the best direction for your organization and sample formats of strategic plans are described on pages 52-69.

Step 4: Refine and Adopt the Plan

The next step is to refine or tune up the draft plan and secure necessary approvals. In this step the first draft—if it seems generally on target— is sharpened to increase the likelihood of successful implementation and ensure broad-based commitment. Pages 70-71 contain tips for reviewing, refining, and approving your strategic plan.

Figure 3:
**Steps to Develop
a Strategic Plan**

*Note: A one-page
version of this figure
suitable for photo-
copying and use in
staff and board
meetings can be
found on page 131.*

**STEP 1
Get Organized**

**STEP 2
Take Stock
(Situation Analysis)**

- Note why you are planning and any concerns
- Select a steering group or person to keep the planning on track
- Determine if outside help is needed
- Outline the planning process that fits your organization
- Get commitment to proceed

- Pull together necessary background information
- Review your nonprofit's past, present, and future situation
- Identify key issues or choices

Step 5: Implement the Plan

A good plan needs good implementation. In Step 5 the organization implements the plan, periodically monitors progress, makes adjustments, then updates the plan—usually every one to three years. Suggestions for implementing your plan, monitoring progress, and updating the plan are outlined on pages 72-74.

How do you adapt these five steps to fit your nonprofit? Pages 16-18 will show you how to do this step-by-step. But here are two general tips: (1) design a planning process that you can realistically complete, and (2) stay focused on the most critical issues and concerns.

STEP 3 Set Direction	STEP 4 Refine and Adopt the Plan	STEP 5 Implement the Plan

- Develop a vision of your organization's future
  - Critical issues approach
  - Scenario approach
  - Goals approach
  - Alignment approach
- Determine how to move the organization toward this future
- Develop a first draft of the plan

- Review and refine the plan
- Adopt the plan

- Implement the plan
- Monitor progress
- Make adjustments
- Periodically update the plan

Design a Planning Process That Is Realistic

We suggest that you design a strategic planning process that your organization will be able to complete without getting sidetracked or lost. This means taking into account factors such as the following.

Your experience with planning

If you have never developed a strategic plan, we suggest that you get some guidance before proceeding—not just from this book, but from other publications listed in the bibliography, from someone experienced with such planning, from similar organizations that have done a good job with their planning, or from a course or workshop on the subject. We usually suggest that groups new to strategic planning use a relatively simple, straightforward process to develop their first plan. The second time through (usually a year or two later), you may want to use a more involved approach. With experience, your organization can expect to get better at planning.

The time available

Beware of designing a planning process that will take forty hours of meeting time when you know that ten to fifteen hours is as much time as you can realistically expect from your staff or board. This can lead to frustration and failure. Effective strategic planning can be done in as little as ten to fifteen hours of meeting time, with good preparation between meetings. However, some organizations—for example, larger nonprofits whose planning involves several managerial layers, or organizations with broad-based constituencies—may prefer a slower, more deliberate process. As you design your planning process, consider whether a short, quick-moving process or a slower, more deliberate process will work better for you. Outline the process you will use, then check to see that the time required is realistic for staff, board, and others. If not, make adjustments before proceeding.

Leadership

Often, several kinds of leadership are needed in strategic planning—for example, from a steering group or person to keep the overall planning on track, from the executive and staff in suggesting future program options or financial strategies, from the board in suggesting and evaluating major shifts in direction, or from a consultant in suggesting appropriate planning methods or facilitating certain meetings. When designing your planning process, we suggest that you outline the major steps and note who will be responsible for facilitating or leading each step. If you anticipate a problem at any point (from group dynamics, missing information, or other reasons), find a way to address it.

Commitment of your organization's leaders is critical to developing and implementing a good strategic plan. Involve leaders deeply. If key people or groups are wary of the planning, find out why and address these concerns. Several factors can help build commitment: a clear reason for planning, a process that makes sense, good use of people's time and talents, a feeling of progress as you proceed, and people's personal connection with what's being proposed.

Number of people and groups involved

Strategic planning processes also differ according to the number of people and groups involved. Some nonprofits prefer to involve primarily board and key staff in developing their plan. Other nonprofits prefer to involve many additional constituencies (for example, service users, potential partners, community groups, experts in the field, funders, and others). Still other organizations prefer something in between. Engaging wider groups of people in the planning can contribute greatly to the quality of the plan and others' support, but note that such involvement usually adds time, expense, and complexity. Pages 29-32 offer several tips for making these decisions.

Mini-plans

Most nonprofits develop one strategic plan which serves as a guide for the entire organization. In addition, some organizations like to develop separate strategic plans for each of their major divisions or programs, which tie into the overall plan. Often, such mini-plans are developed when a nonprofit's major divisions or programs function somewhat separately. For example, through its planning, a large decentralized human service agency determined that a shift in focus was needed. Each of its three divisions developed a strategic plan (mini-plan) describing how this new focus would be implemented. The division plans were then incorporated into the nonprofit's overall strategic plan.

Technical and political issues

Technical or political issues also need to be taken into account in shaping a good planning process. On technical questions, you need enough information to make a well-informed decision. For example, your nonprofit may be debating whether to develop an on-site day care but you know little about the associated regulations. Before making a final decision, you may need to find someone familiar with the day care field to advise you on possible regulations and financing options.

Also, there are often issues of a political or intergroup nature that arise in planning, like needing the cooperation of a key community group. In laying out your planning process, consider how such groups might be appropriately involved.

Focus on Critical Issues

A second general tip about tailoring a strategic planning process to fit your nonprofit is to make sure that the planning stays focused on the most critical issues or choices facing your organization. Large quantities of planning time can be wasted on issues and information which are not central to your organization's future. Studies of effective leadership and successful innovation stress the importance of keeping people's attention focused on the most promising ideas and the most critical issues. Examples of critical issues may be: "How can we shape our services to better address a particular community condition or achieve a better outcome?" or "How will we cope with the expected cut in our largest source of funding?" or "Should we pursue an alliance or partnership with another organization which has complementary strengths?"

Good attention to the first three steps of your planning—*Get Organized, Take Stock,* and *Set Direction*—will help the planning stay focused and on track. If at any point your planning begins to wander, note that this is occurring and discuss how to get back to the central strategic issues or choices.

Section I Summary

Section II of the workbook is designed to help you develop a strategic plan step-by-step. As you proceed, four summary tips may be helpful:

- At its core, strategic planning is developing an orienting vision that guides your next steps.

  Actively engage people in clarifying what your nonprofit hopes to accomplish and how you will accomplish these goals. Then keep moving toward that future, and adjust your plans as you learn what works.

- Keep your planning simple, unless there's a good reason to make it more complex.

- Stay focused on the important things.

- Four ingredients are critical to developing a good plan: getting good ideas on the table, making good decisions about how to proceed, developing a shared understanding of and commitment to the directions chosen, and a plan which has some heart.

By "a plan which has some heart" we mean planning in which partici-pants speak candidly about their hopes for the organization and what it can accomplish, their commitments, and other matters of heart. A strate-gic plan has little power if it is disconnected from people's hopes and com-mitments. The difference between an adequate plan and a great plan is often around these matters. As an astute minister noted, "What goes deepest to the heart goes widest to the world." This applies to individuals, groups of citizens, nonprofit organizations, and larger movements as well.

Developing Your Strategic Plan

Introduction

This section is a step-by-step guide for developing a strategic plan for your organization. The pages that follow will:

- Describe each of the five planning steps

- Offer tips on how to undertake each step

- Provide examples that may aid you in your planning

Section IV, Worksheets, on pages 109-129 contains blank worksheets which may be useful in organizing your strategic planning process and collecting information from participants. You can copy the worksheets which you find most useful.

A community-based development organization named N.E.A.R. (North End Area Revitalization) is used in this section to illustrate how one organization organized its strategic planning. N.E.A.R. was founded in 1984 to revitalize an ailing commercial district in an urban neighborhood of St. Paul, Minnesota. At that time, 40 percent of the commercial space in the neighborhood's primary business district was vacant. After very hard work and planning by N.E.A.R. and others, that vacancy rate was lowered to and has remained under 10 percent. N.E.A.R. is also used as an example at other points in this workbook, and its strategic plan is included in Appendix B.

Step 1: Get Organized

The major task in Step 1 is to organize your strategic planning process. Your task is to lay out a planning process that results in a good plan, builds commitment, and uses people's time well. Poor groundwork in Step 1 can result in wasted time, frustration, and low-quality plans. In Step 1 you will:

- Note why you are planning and any concerns
- Select a steering group or person to keep the planning on track
- Determine if outside help is needed
- Outline a planning process that fits your organization
- Get commitment of key people to proceed

Note Why You Are Planning and Any Concerns

Before beginning to plan, pause for a moment to consider why you are planning and to note any concerns you have. First consider the benefits or payoffs you anticipate from the planning. For example, do you hope that the planning will solve a growing financial problem, lead to a renewed sense of mission for your agency, improve your nonprofit's effectiveness in serving your community, or help you decide whether to expand? The benefits listed on pages 9-10 of this book may stimulate your thinking.

On the other hand, what are your concerns about strategic planning? For example, are you unsure how to organize the planning effort? Are you concerned that staff or board members will not devote the necessary time? Did your last attempt at strategic planning derail? Does this seem like a bad time to undertake such a planning effort? Note any concerns and ways you might steer around each of them.

Weighing the possible benefits of strategic planning against any concerns, what is the wisest course of action?

- Proceed with strategic planning—full steam ahead
- Proceed with caution, addressing any concerns
- Wait until a better time to begin
- Stop—don't proceed

List the benefits you expect from strategic planning as well as any concerns you have. Worksheet 1, Benefits and Concerns, on page 111 may be a useful tool. Decide with other leaders of your organization how you will proceed with your planning.

TASK

Here's how N.E.A.R. used Worksheet 1 to identify the benefits it hoped to receive from planning, as well as concerns:

WORKSHEET 1 — Benefits and Concerns

INSTRUCTIONS

1. List the benefits you expect from strategic planning as well as any concerns.
2. Note possible ways to build benefits and overcome concerns. Circle the best ideas.
3. Decide how you will proceed.

Benefits expected	Concerns	Ways to build benefits and overcome concerns
1) Continue to make it happen in the North End. 2) Clarify N.E.A.R.'s future role and priorities.	1) Attendance has been down some at recent board meetings. 2) Would be good to get the thoughts and suggestions from the Neighborhood Housing Agenda Committee and the Community Building Initiative Committee.	1) Review the planning process with board members and stress importance of everyone being at the retreat. Do our best to pick a time when everyone can attend. 2) Hold focus group discussions with each of the two committees before the retreat—also ask members to complete planning questionnaires if they wish.

Decide how you will proceed

- ☑ Full steam ahead
- ☐ With caution, addressing the concerns above
- ☐ Wait until a better time to begin
- ☐ Stop— don't proceed

Select a Steering Group or Person to Keep the Planning on Track

Most organizations either select a steering group or designate an individual to oversee the strategic planning and keep it on track. A steering group often includes the executive director and one or more board representatives. Key staff are also sometimes included. Occasionally other constituents are represented on the committee. The steering group's job is to outline the proposed planning process, select and oversee any consultants, and recommend adjustments in the planning process if they are needed. In addition, the steering group often oversees the drafting and revisions of the plan. A consultant may assist the steering group with its work.

Another approach is to designate one person to coordinate the planning and keep it on track. This person is usually the executive director, a board member with experience in planning who works closely with the executive, a staff person with expertise in planning, or a consultant. If a staff person or consultant coordinates the planning, the executive director customarily oversees that work.

TASK

> Determine whether to use a steering group or appoint an individual to guide the planning. Ask those people to serve.

Determine If Outside Help Is Needed

A third issue in organizing your planning is deciding whether you need outside help in designing the planning process or in completing any of the planning steps. Several kinds of resources could be useful:

- Books or articles on strategic planning

- Courses and seminars

- Consultants or advisors—a planning consultant or resource person on specific issues

- Other organizations which have created successful strategic plans

Books or articles

If you have never developed a strategic plan, a good book or article on the subject can be useful. In addition to this workbook, the publications listed in the bibliography on pages 105-108 contain much helpful information.

Courses and seminars

Courses, seminars, or workshops on strategic planning are available in most major cities. Check with universities, management training organizations, organizations like United Way, or professional groups. In many cities, technical assistance organizations offer workshops on strategic planning geared to nonprofit groups.

Consultants or advisors

Some organizations use paid or volunteer consultants to assist with planning. A skilled planning consultant can help keep your planning focused and on track. A consultant or facilitator can free organizational leaders to be participants in meetings without having to manage the agenda or discussion. On the other hand, an organization can rely too heavily on a consultant so that the plan becomes the consultant's and not the organization's. Consultants sometimes cost money you do not have. Asking an experienced planner to volunteer his or her time is an option.

There are several ways that planning consultants or facilitators might help:

- Assist in designing the planning process
- Orient or train participants
- Assist in gathering or summarizing data
- Facilitate or summarize meetings
- Lead you through the whole strategic planning process
- Coach the steering group or person who is leading the process
- Advise you on specific questions related to strategic planning or technical issues such as the format of plans, making financial projections, or how to investigate new program options
- Provide advice on process or technical issues
- Provide other advice or assistance if you get stuck

You may need help in only one or two of the areas above. Or you may not need a planning consultant at all. If you do use one, be clear about what you expect and what his or her role will be. Remember that the consultant is there to serve you.

Some nonprofits also use other kinds of advisors in their planning. For example, you may want to involve someone who can give an overview of issues or trends in your community or field. Or if you are considering a new program approach or financing strategy, you might want to bring in someone who can inform you about that approach. If asked, many people will volunteer their time to make a one-shot presentation. As above, be as clear as you can with resource people about what you would like them to do.

Other organizations

Another source of help is other organizations which have done good strategic planning. Find out how they did their planning and what they learned. In addition to information on how they conducted their strategic planning, other organizations sometimes have information about your field or the community that can be very helpful in your planning, or such organizations might be potential partners in implementing your plan.

TASK

Decide if you need assistance in developing your plan. If you want help in designing the planning process, find a capable resource. If you need other assistance, note this as you complete Worksheet 2, Organize the Planning Effort, on pages 113-115.

Outline a Planning Process That Fits Your Organization

The primary task in organizing your strategic planning is to outline a process that will produce a good plan that people are committed to implementing. That process should be tailored to fit your organization. In Section I we suggested two keys to developing a planning process that will work well for you:

- Be realistic about practical matters such as your experience with planning and the time available.

- Keep the planning focused on the most critical issues or choices facing your organization.

The five-step model introduced on pages 14-15 can easily be adapted to fit your nonprofit. Strategic plans can be developed relatively quickly—for example, through a four- to six-hour retreat with information about key issues gathered beforehand, followed by two to three briefer meetings to draft and review the plan. Quicker can be better. Focused planning, which keeps moving at a fairly quick pace, often produces a better plan than a more leisurely, drawn-out process which can tend to wander. Some nonprofit organizations, however, prefer to slow down their planning to allow time for more data gathering, very deliberate and complete discussions, and the development of plans across several layers of the organization. If you prefer a more complex planning process, make sure that you have a clear reason for including each planning step and that you can see how information and decisions from each step will mesh to produce a final plan.

Examples of the strategic planning processes used by two nonprofit organizations are provided in Figures 4 and 5 on pages 30-31.

Figure 4 outlines the process recently used by N.E.A.R., which preferred a fairly compact, quick-moving strategic planning approach requiring about five months to complete.

Figure 5 outlines the strategic planning process used by a large human service organization. Through planning, this organization determined that a different approach was required to better serve its community. The organization decided to emphasize working in partnership with neighborhoods, residents, other nonprofits, and government to help build the capacities of urban families and neighborhoods. The organization preferred a more extended, fifteen-month planning process that gave time for its three major divisions to consider how to implement this new focus in partnership with the people and groups noted above. The executive director and board chair provided general oversight of the planning.

In assisting organizations to design their planning process, we are frequently asked, "What people and groups should be involved—and when?" Organizations often select: (1) a planning approach which relies primarily on the organization's board and staff to generate ideas and make decisions; (2) an approach that involves a much wider range of the organization's stakeholders; or (3) an approach in between these two—one that selectively involves critical people or groups at key points in the planning. As you decide who to involve, we suggest you consider:

- Whose ideas and support are needed to develop and implement the plan? What people and groups might be involved—for example, board members, staff, service users, community groups, experts in your field, funders, potential partners, and so on?

- At what stages of the planning might each group be meaningfully involved—for example, in *Getting Organized, Taking Stock, Setting Direction, Refining and Adopting the Plan, Implementing the Plan?*

- How could each group's ideas, opinions, or support be best solicited at those points—for example, by representation on the steering group; by review of the planning process; by being interviewed, completing a questionnaire, or attending a focus group session; through participation in one or more planning or review meetings; or by being asked to provide leadership in implementing part of the plan?

- Practical factors in completing a plan—for example, the time available, how simple or complex a planning process you can handle right now, expense, or confidentiality concerns.

Figure 4: N.E.A.R.'s Strategic Planning Process

Steps	Responsible	By When
1. Select a steering group. (The board's executive committee and executive director served in this role.)	Board chair and executive director	Feb. 1
2. Select a consultant to assist in design and facilitation of this process.	Steering group	Feb. 15
3. Get agreement on the planning steps, responsibilities, and resources required.	Steering group, consultant	Feb. 25
4. Gather information via a questionnaire from board members, staff, other neighborhood representatives, and others familiar with N.E.A.R.—regarding our image, strengths, weaknesses, opportunities, and critical issues/choices. Also conduct focus group discussions with staff, the Neighborhood Housing Agenda Committee, and Community Building Initiative Committee about their hopes for the future and issues that need attention in the planning. Summarize this information.	Consultant, staff, steering group	March 20
5. At a six-hour planning retreat with board and staff: • Review N.E.A.R.'s history and accomplishments since inception; note when participants got involved and what lessons they've learned. Use timeline. • Review progress toward our mission and goals over the past year. • Review summary of questionnaire responses and information on neighborhood changes. In small groups, identify key issues or choices for N.E.A.R. • Determine N.E.A.R.'s future direction, using the alignment approach. (See page 59 of workbook for for a description of the alignment approach.) • Review steps to complete the strategic plan.	Participants, consultant	April 1
6. Summarize the retreat.	Consultant, executive director	April 12
7. At two follow-up meetings (approximately two hours each), develop a draft of the strategic plan. The executive director will develop the initial draft for discussion and refinement with the steering group.	Steering group, consultant as needed	May 15
8. Review the draft with staff, board, other community representatives, and a key funder. Make needed revisions based on these reviews.	Steering group, consultant as needed	June 10
9. Approve the plan.	Board	June 25
10. Implement the plan.	Those indicated	July 1
11. Monitor progress at six months and update the plan yearly.	Steering group	Feb. 1

Meeting time required:

Approximately eighteen to twenty hours for steps one through eight, plus staff work in preparing for the retreat and drafting the plan.

Figure 5: Longer Planning Process of a Large Human Service Organization

Steps	Responsible	By When
1. Get agreement on planning steps, responsibilities, and timelines. Review the planning process with the board and staff.	Executive director and board chair	Feb. 1
2. Meet informally with neighborhood groups, user groups, other nonprofits, public officials, funders, and others to solicit ideas on how our organization might better serve this community. Summarize this information.	Executive director and designated staff	May 1
3. In preparation for the board/management planning retreat, summarize information on: (1) the organization's mission, success, and limitations over the past twenty years; (2) human service and community trends; and (3) several options and scenarios for how the organization might have greatest impact in coming years.	Executive director with staff support	July 1
4. At a two-day board/management retreat, review and discuss the information above and determine the organization's future focus and emphasis. Use scenario approach. Invite two resource people with knowledge of these issues to participate in the retreat. (See page 55 of workbook for a description of the scenario approach.)	Participants, guests, facilitator	Aug. 1
5. Summarize the retreat, develop a proposed focus statement for the organization, and discuss implications with staff.	Executive director, management staff	Sept. 15
6. Review implications and approve the focus statement.	Board	Oct. 15
7. Draft strategic plans for each of the organization's three divisions describing how they will implement the new focus over the next five years. Involve potential partner groups in developing these plans.	Executive director, management staff	Jan. 1
8. Review division plans. Note any recommended changes, areas that require coordination across the organization, and implications for administrative support services.	Executive director, management staff	Jan. 15
9. Draft overall strategic plan for the organization.	Executive director	March 1
10. Review draft plan with staff, the board, and six to eight community representatives. Make revisions based on these reviews.	Executive director	April 1
11. Approve strategic plan.	Board	May 1
12. Implement the plan. Review progress and update the plan yearly.	Executive director and those indicated	

Meeting time required:

Sixty to sixty-five hours for steps one through ten (includes strategic planning for each division), plus staff time for informal meetings with community representatives, development of background materials for the retreat, and drafting the plan.

The steering group or person coordinating the planning outlines a strategic planning process using some variation of the five-step process described in this workbook—including who will be involved at each step. The proposed planning process is usually reviewed with the board and staff before beginning—to see if there are additional suggestions.

Worksheet 2, Organize the Planning Process, is designed to help you adapt this five-step planning model to fit your organization. If you are using a planning consultant, he or she can offer suggestions. (Note: Because this worksheet requires that you have an overall picture of the planning process, we suggest that you read the remainder of this book before completing Worksheet 2.)

TASK

> Review the remainder of this book. Then use Worksheet 2 to outline the process you will use to develop your strategic plan.

An example of how N.E.A.R. thought through its strategic planning process using Worksheet 2 can be found on pages 33-34.

Get Commitment of Key People to Proceed

The commitment of an organization's leaders to planning—particularly the executive director—is critical. Don't begin without it. The commitment of board members and key staff is also very important. When commitment is a problem, the following approaches can be effective.

Get educated

Learn more about strategic planning and how your organization can use it effectively as a tool. This book, a workshop, or an orientation session with a consultant might help.

Discuss benefits and concerns frankly

Discuss specifically what the planning might accomplish—for example, reduce deficits, improve services, clarify whether to merge. Clarity about payoffs can increase interest and motivation. Also discuss any concerns about the planning and how each concern might be addressed. The hesitant person may see a problem that others have missed.

WORSHEET 2 — Organize the Planning Effort

WORKSHEET 2   **Organize the Planning Effort**

INSTRUCTIONS

Indicate how each of the following issues will be handled. Then outline the
steps, responsibilities, and timelines for developing your strategic plan.

1. You are developing a strategic plan for:
   - ☐ Your total organization
   - ☑ Total organization, plus each major program or division
   - ☐ Only part of your organization (a division or program)
   - ☐ A multi-organization initiative or coalition
   - ☐ Other:

2. For what period of time are you planning?
   - ☐ Next 2 years
   - ☑ Next 3 years
   - ☐ Next 4 years
   - ☐ Next 5 years
   - ☐ Other (specify): _____

3. What critical issues do you hope the planning will address?

   1) Continue to make things happen, including business vitality on Rice Street and in other areas.

   2) Clarify N.E.A.R.'s future role with housing and the Community Building Initiative.

   3) Clarify future funding strategies for some program areas.

4. Time devoted to planning: Which approach do you prefer?
   - ☐ "What we can do in a limited time" approach: Under sixteen hours of planning meetings
   - ☑ A compact approach: Sixteen to thirty hours of planning meetings
   - ☐ A more extended approach: More than thirty hours of planning meetings

5. Who will manage the planning effort and keep it on track?
   - ☐ An individual:

   - ☑ A steering group: (suggested members)
     Board's executive committee and the executive director

   - ☐ Other:

6. Are you going to use a consultant or other resource persons in developing the plan?
   - ☑ Yes   ☐ No   ☐ Unsure

   If so, what kind of help do you need?
   (Page 27 has suggestions.)

   1) Advice on the design of the planning process

   2) Help in gathering and summarizing information before a planning retreat

   3) Facilitation of the planning retreat and follow-up meetings

   4) Assist the executive director in developing first draft of plan, if needed

(continued)

WORKSHEET 2—Organize the Planning Effort

7. Note who should be involved in developing the plan. (List people or groups.)
   Note the planning steps in which they should be involved. (Check as many boxes as apply.)

	Step 1: Get Organized	Step 2: Take Stock	Step 3: Set Direction	Step 4: Refine and Adopt the Plan	Step 5: Implement the Plan
Board members	✔	✔	✔	✔	✔
Executive director	✔	✔	✔	✔	✔
Other staff or staff groups:					
All staff	✔	✔	✔	✔	✔
Other stakeholder groups:					
Community representatives (beyond those on the board)		✔		✔	
Neighborhood Housing Agenda and Community Building Initiative committees		✔	✔	✔	
Other local community development people		✔			
Major funders		✔		✔	
Consultants and resource people:					
Planning consultant	✔	✔	✔	✔	

8. By what date do you want to have the plan approved?   five months from now

9. Outline the steps you will use in developing your plan. After outlining the process,
   review it with the people involved. Finally, make any changes needed.

Steps	Responsible	By When

(See Figure 4 on page 30 for an outline of the planning process that N.E.A.R. used.)

Outline planning steps

Leaders sometimes hesitate to commit themselves to a process that is unclear or poorly conceived. Outline the steps you will use to develop the plan. Review the outline with the board and key staff. Ask for suggested improvements. This can build commitment to the planning effort.

Jump in

For some, the only way to build excitement and commitment is to begin, and to ensure that each planning session is productive.

> Review the proposed planning process with those involved. Make any needed adjustments in the process based on those reviews. Get any necessary approval to proceed.

TASK

Step 1 Summary

In Step 1 you have organized your strategic planning effort. Specifically, you have:

- Decided to develop a strategic plan
- Selected a group or person to coordinate the effort
- Outlined a planning process
- Enlisted any outside help needed
- Gotten necessary approval to proceed

As you proceed, you may need to adjust your planning process to address new issues that emerge. The work you've done in Step 1 should help the next steps of the planning go smoothly.

In Step 2 you will take stock of your organization's history, present situation, and future possibilities.

Step 2: Take Stock
(Situation Analysis)

Your task in Step 2 is to take a hard look at your organization and the world in which you operate, and then identify key issues or choices regarding your organiza-tion's future. We call this step "Taking Stock." In strategic planning jargon, Step 2 is often called a "situation analysis." If done well, your planning discussion in Step 2 will result in a clear, common understanding of your organization's situation as well as a clear definition of the strategic issues and choices the organization faces. Worksheets 3-7 are provided to help you through Step 2.

How do you begin? Many nonprofit organizations proceed with their situation analysis in three stages:

- Pull together the background information necessary to have a good discussion of your organization's situation.

- Hold one or more planning meetings to discuss your nonprofit's past, present, and possible future. The discussion often focuses on your organization's history and recent progress, mission, internal strengths and weaknesses, and external opportunities and threats.

- Toward the end of this discussion, get agreement on the most critical issues or choices regarding your organization's future.

Many nonprofits like to proceed through this Step 2 discussion in a me-thodical, step-by-step manner—first gathering the background informa-tion needed, then examining each of the dimensions noted above (history, recent progress, mission, and so on), then agreeing on what the major stra-tegic issues or choices are. Other nonprofits prefer a more streamlined or targeted approach in Step 2.

Following are tips on how to take stock of your organization's situation using the basic, step-by-step approach. Ways to streamline this review are noted on page 51.

Pull Together Necessary Background Information

Your first task in Step 2 is to pull together information that will help you have a useful discussion of your nonprofit's past, present, and future situation. You first decide what information will be useful, and then choose the best way to collect it. Gather enough information to make well-informed decisions, but not so much that you get lost. Some of this information is usually collected before the full planning group meets, and other information is gathered in the planning meetings.

Information gathered beforehand can come from such methods as:

- Conversations, interviews, or group discussions (focus groups, community meetings)—for example, with your organization's stakeholders and other resource people.

- Worksheets or questionnaires.

- Analysis of existing information—for example, from organizational records or other reports.

- Organizational assessments.

- Literature review, professional conferences, or site visits—for example, to examine new approaches in your field.

We are not suggesting that you use all of these methods. Pick only those that make sense to you and fit the character of your organization. Look ahead to how the planning process will proceed. Then consider the background information that needs to be gathered and summarized beforehand in order to have a useful discussion. Use Worksheets 3-7 to gather this background information, or use other information-gathering methods if they fit better.

After you collect this background information, summarize it in a way that can be easily understood by planning group members. On questionnaire summaries you may wish to list people's word-for-word responses, grouping similar responses under several headings. Or you can simply note the common themes that emerge from the information collected.

Here are examples of how two nonprofits gathered background information before their strategic planning retreats.

A community development corporation

In preparation for its "taking-stock" discussion, Neighborhood Development Center—which provides micro-entrepreneur training and loans across thirteen neighborhoods—first held a meeting with board and staff to review the proposed planning process. A planning questionnaire was then sent to board members, staff, a sample of entrepreneurs, neighborhood partners, and several other respected people. The questionnaire asked the following questions:

1) What are your image and overall impressions of Neighborhood Development Center?

2) What do you see us doing well? What are our strengths?

3) Where do we need to improve?

4) What opportunities or challenges do you see for the Neighborhood Development Center over the next two to three years?

5) What role(s), initiatives, or programs can you imagine the Neighborhood Development Center pursuing in coming months and years?

6) What relationships may be important for us to develop or nurture?

7) Are there any other ideas or issues that we should consider in our planning?

In addition, several kinds of program, financial, and administrative information from the last three years were summarized in preparing for the planning retreat: evaluation/success data on the training and loan programs, demographic information, comparable success information on similar organizations, an outside review of Neighborhood Development Center's program policies and administrative systems, and an overall summary of progress versus goals. A national expert on community economic development was also asked to speak on trends in the field and participate in the retreat.

An urban youth-serving group

An inner-city youth-serving organization with a widely representative board uses a simpler method of preparation for "take-stock" discussions at its yearly strategic planning retreat. Board members and key staff complete a planning questionnaire. The executive director also pulls together summary information on the past year's progress toward the goals noted in the organization's strategic plan. The board and key staff then discuss this information as one step in updating the strategic plan each year.

TASK

Determine what information needs to be gathered before your "take-stock" discussion. Gather that information and summarize it in usable form. Worksheets 3-7 on pages 117-129 or a questionnaire like that used by Neighborhood Development Center in the example above can be used to gather much of this information.

Review Your Nonprofit's Past, Present, and Future Situation

Once background information is assembled, it is time to take stock of the organization. At a retreat or series of planning meetings, a planning group (often composed of board, staff representatives, and possibly others) reviews and discusses their nonprofit's history, recent progress, current mission, strengths, weaknesses, opportunities, and threats. Finally, the group agrees on the most critical issues or choices facing the organization. That review often proceeds as follows.

History and development over time

Some board members, staff, and other participants in the planning may not know the history of your organization very well. A clear understanding of your nonprofit's history—such as why it was established, its stages of development, important values—can be very helpful in charting a future direction that builds upon your historic strengths and values.

We often ask one or more people to make a presentation which covers:

- The organization's beginning: start-up, original mission and services, key people
- Significant changes, events, and people since start-up

Participants can add other significant events. Sometimes a timeline is used, on which participants indicate major events and milestones for the organization. Then historic strengths, values, and lessons are often noted—particularly strengths that people hope to carry into the future. For example, after reviewing its history, the leadership of one organization determined that two values had been critical to its past success: the ability to deliver (the organization had helped bring a long string of improvements to the neighborhood), and the importance of building broad community involvement and support. Planning participants felt that these two values should be prominent in their new strategic plan.

In reviewing your organization's history, you may also find it useful to discuss your nonprofit's stages of development over time. For example, after reviewing its history, one nonprofit noted four significant stages in its development: a start-up period which was characterized by struggle, a period of rapid growth, a more stable period when that growth was digested, and the present—a time of decision about the wisdom of further expansion.

Each stage of a nonprofit's development or growth can bring predictable challenges. Start-up periods often bring issues related to building basic services, a funding base, and other support for the organization, as well as getting basic administrative systems in place. As the organization grows, people beyond the founder often need to provide more leadership, funds need to be secured for expansion, and efforts need to be made to ensure consistent quality. These steps help the organization outgrow its original ways of doing things. In a period of stability there may be issues around creativity or "fire." Organizations in an institution-building mode may face issues around building a different kind of board or forming alliances. Organizations that are in a time of decline may find it difficult to keep people's eyes on the mission and to address changes head-on.

In reviewing your organization's history, take a few minutes to discuss your nonprofit's development over time, and then note any developmental issues that will likely need attention.

WORKSHEET 3   History and Present Situation

INSTRUCTIONS

1. Review your organization's history and present situation.
2. List any historical issues or trends that will need attention as you plan for the future.

1) Historically N.E.A.R. was formed to revitalize the ailing Rice Street commercial district. We've made good progress by persistently working on the commercial vitality of Rice Street. Will work on other commercial locations in the neighborhood, housing, and youth diffuse us too much?

2) Our credibility and reputation have remained strong over the years. We need to keep earning our reputation.

3) Leadership development has been a critical part of all our activities.

Recent progress

In addition to reviewing their nonprofit's past, many organizations also find it helpful to review their recent progress—particularly if they have a current strategic plan or yearly organizational goals in place. The executive director (or other staff) often begins this discussion by referencing the organization's current goals, then commenting on progress in achieving those goals over the past one to two years. She or he may also comment on lessons learned during that period. This is also an opportunity for the executive to highlight any issues that need particular attention in the planning.

After this presentation, we usually invite other planning group participants to share their thoughts about the organization's recent progress. We often ask a question like, "On a scale of one to ten, with ten being *fantastic progress* toward accomplishing our mission and one being *moving backward,* how would you rate the organization's progress over the past year?" We record people's responses and then ask them to comment (if they wish) on their ratings, recording the major points raised. This method very quickly brings to the surface key issues that will need to be addressed later in the planning.

Worksheet 3, History and Present Situation, on page 117 can be used to collect information on your nonprofit's history and current situation. (The example on page 40 shows how N.E.A.R. completed Worksheet 3.)

Current mission

Many nonprofit organizations also like to review their current mission as part of "taking stock." An organization's mission is its statement of basic purpose or reason for existence. In its most simple form, that mission describes what organizational leaders hope to accomplish in the long run: "What good do we hope to accomplish with whom?" For example, the mission of a prenatal health program may be "to increase child and maternal health among families in Baxter County." Or the mission of a community development organization may be "to improve the economic, social, and cultural vitality on the West Side." Developing a shared understanding of your organization's future mission, purpose, or basic goal is a critical part of strategic planning.

Mission Statements

Many organizations prefer to have one simple statement of mission. Other nonprofits prefer to have two or three statements to guide them.[1] For example, some organizations develop a brief *vision or purpose statement* (what they are committed to accomplishing), a brief *business statement* (the main methods or activities they will use to achieve their purpose), and a *values statement* (core values that will guide the organization). The International Youth Foundation, a youth development organization, uses this framework to describe its vision, business, and values as follows:[2]

- *Vision: What We're Committed To*
  To improve the conditions and prospects for children and youth where they live, learn, work, and play.

- *Mission: What's Our Business*
  To identify, strengthen, and expand effective programs that promote positive youth development and to encourage greater understanding and application of knowledge about "what works" for young people.

- *Values: What We Believe*
  Young people are a global priority and have the innate right to develop their full potential to become responsible and caring adults. Every young person should be entitled to a standard of living adequate for healthy development; and to a quality education. Every young person should be protected from economic, sexual, and physical exploitation that is likely to be hazardous or which interferes with his or her education, or which is harmful to his or her physical, mental, spiritual, moral, or social development. Young people should care for their communities and communities should care for their young people.

If this three-step framework is not helpful or confusing to you, we suggest that you stick with one simple statement of your organization's mission, which describes what good you hope to accomplish.

Nonprofits often use questions like the following to review their mission: "Is our mission clear? Is it well stated? Are there parts of our mission statement that you wonder about? Might our mission need to change in the future?" The meeting facilitator or scribe records people's responses to each question, those responses are discussed, and then the group agrees on the issues or questions about mission that will need further attention. If your nonprofit does not have a formal mission statement, you can have a similar discussion about the organization's basic purpose or goal.

After noting people's ideas about the current mission, some nonprofits like to go ahead and revise their mission statement, if needed. That approach can work; however, we usually suggest that organizations wait until Step 3 of the planning process (Set Direction) to make revisions in their mission statement. By the middle of Step 3, you have had a chance to explore a number of options concerning your future direction and focus. The task in Step 2 is simply to explore the questions you have about your organization's mission.

Worksheet 4, Questions about Mission, on page 119 can be used to examine your organization's mission statement. The example below shows how N.E.A.R. used Worksheet 4.

WORKSHEET 4   Questions about Mission

INSTRUCTIONS
1. Describe below your understanding of your organization's mission or purpose.
2. List any questions, ideas, or concerns you have about your present mission.
3. Note any ideas about how your organization's mission could or should change.

Present mission or purpose

Improve the North End community through economic development efforts that strengthen the local economy, improve the image of the neighborhood, and increase employment opportunities for area residents.

Questions about the current mission

1) How do N.E.A.R.'s newer programs, which focus on housing and youth, fit with or complement our historic focus on the commercial development of Rice Street? Where should our future emphasis be?

2) Our mission statement may need to be revised to reflect N.E.A.R.'s expanded community development role.

Possible changes in the mission for the future

1) Broaden mission from current economic development focus to "community and economic development."

2) Consider adding language about our goal of building neighborhood capacity for broad-based community renewal.

Strengths and weaknesses

A clear understanding of your organization's resources and capabilities—or lack thereof—is critical to developing a good strategic plan. Resources and capabilities can include staff, board, expertise, finances, relationships, goodwill, facilities, and any other resources necessary to accomplish your goals.

A candid assessment of strengths and weaknesses will help you identify strengths to build on, vulnerabilities in your organization, and new capabilities that are needed. For example, one nonprofit determined that its primary strengths were a strong dedication to the organization's mission, a highly motivated and skilled staff, and a very good track record of helping unemployed people get and keep jobs. On the other hand, the planning group discovered that the organization had outgrown its original administrative systems, new staff were not being adequately oriented and trained, and a strained relationship with another organization was sapping much of management's energy and attention. Later in the planning (in Step 3), the organization determined how to keep building on those historic strengths and remedy the three problems that had been identified.

After you develop an initial list of your organization's strengths and weaknesses (for example, using Worksheet 5, a questionnaire, or a brainstorming session), we suggest you review this information with the planning group. Many groups use questions like the following to guide this discussion:

- Are there other major strengths which should be added to the list?
- Which are our greatest strengths?
- Are we mobilizing these strengths well?
- Are there other strengths we need for the future?

And . . .

- Are there other weaknesses, vulnerabilities, or capability gaps that should be added to the list?
- Are these weaknesses significant or minor?
- Which seem to hold us back the most?
- How might we build needed capabilities?

Work with participants to get agreement on strengths that need to be tapped and developed in coming months, and the weaknesses that most need mending. Worksheet 5, Strengths and Weaknesses, on page 121 (example on page 45) can be used to record strengths and weaknesses.

WORKSHEET 5 — Strengths and Weaknesses

INSTRUCTIONS

1. List the major strengths and weaknesses of your organization as it faces the future.
2. Note which strengths and weaknesses will be most critical to your organization's future success.

Strengths and assets	Weaknesses and liabilities
1) N.E.A.R.'s track record, credibility, and reputation	1) Less progress with light industrial development than in other areas
2) Capable board and staff (though some staff are new in their roles)	2) Staff workloads may be getting too great. We may need to add staff or set clearer priorities.
3) Strong support from business owners and funders	3) Need to improve internal systems – computerization, fringe benefits, etc.

Opportunities and threats

The planning group also looks outside the organization to examine major opportunities and threats. These might be related to the people and communities the organization serves; possible competitors or allies; and other major forces (economic, political, social, cultural, technological) which could influence whether the organization succeeds or fails. The task here is not to identify every possible need, opportunity, threat, or force which could possibly influence the organization, but to zero in on a limited number of opportunities or forces (usually four to eight) that will most affect the organization's future.

As noted above, this step in the planning sometimes involves extensive data collection or market research. In some cases, organizations feel familiar enough with their world to rely on their planning participants to identify major opportunities and threats. Worksheet 6, Opportunities and Threats, on pages 123-128 or a questionnaire similar to the one described on page 38 is often used.

After developing an initial list of opportunities and threats, discuss the list in the planning group, add other important issues, and then narrow it down to a smaller list of the most significant opportunities or threats.

One technique for whittling down the list is to divide the number of items on the list by three, and then give people that number of votes. (For example, if there are eighteen possible opportunities and threats, ask everyone to vote for the six that seem most important.) This approach will help you quickly identify and agree on the most significant opportunities and threats.

In identifying the external forces that may influence your nonprofit's future, you might consider three kinds of forces: *customers and other stakeholders*; *competitors and allies*; and *social, cultural, economic, political, and technological forces*.

1. Customers and Other Stakeholders

Research and conventional wisdom indicate that successful organizations stay close to the people they serve. Such organizations are effective at shaping their services, programs, and products to address their constituents' hopes and needs. In addition, others may have a stake in what you do—for example, funders, regulators, or community groups. Do these groups present particular opportunities or threats for the future?

2. Competitors and Allies

Virtually every nonprofit competes for something—for example, funding, people served, or public attention. Your analysis of opportunities and threats should also focus on your organization's distinctive role or competitive position in your community. Generally speaking, where are you strong or vulnerable compared with organizations that do similar things? Why would people prefer to go to your organization rather than some other group?

Nonprofits in highly competitive fields may wish to spend more time in Step 2 on questions like:

- For what do we compete?
- With whom do we compete?
- What are our competitive advantages or weaknesses (for example—quality, results, cost, ability to tailor services, or other unique features)?

Competition sometimes forces nonprofits to become clearer about their unique contribution to their community. For example, one nonprofit that operated a number of fitness programs started losing members when an attractive new recreation and fitness facility opened right down the street. The leaders of the nonprofit concluded that in their current building they would be unable to match the quality of fitness programs offered by the new fitness center. This situation also forced them to reexamine their mission. They decided that "fitness" should not be their organization's central focus in the future. Instead, they could bring the most benefit to the community by helping a segment of the city's population through very difficult life transitions.

Do you need a more in-depth analysis of your competitors? Worksheet 6a, Customers and Other Stakeholders, and Worksheet 6b, Competitors and Allies, on pages 125-128 may help you do a competitive analysis.

On the other hand, other organizations need not be viewed as competitors or threats. Many nonprofits prefer to approach their work from the perspective of: "Who in the community has something to contribute, and how can we work together to improve this community?" These organizations often team up with other nonprofits, residents, community groups, government, and businesses to pursue better solutions to community problems or to address particular needs.

Sometimes organizations that have historically worked in isolation decide that their approach must change. For example, a human service organization which had traditionally worked alone to serve persons with physical disabilities decided that future success required that the organization team up with leaders from this population, employers, government funders, and other groups working to improve conditions for disabled persons in society.

More nonprofits are also considering various ways to merge or network their organizations to gain advantages associated with size, stronger services, lower overhead, or new contracting options. These organizations sometimes use strategic planning methods such as future search conferences, community planning, or appreciative inquiry (described in Appendix A, pages 79-85) to consider how to work together to achieve common goals. At a minimum you should ask, "Are there new ways that our nonprofit can team up with others to achieve common goals?"

3. Social, Cultural, Economic, Political, and Technological Forces

Opportunities and threats also come from other areas:

- Social or cultural—demographic changes, social or cultural trends
- Economic—new funding patterns, economic trends
- Political—new legislation, changes in leadership or political philosophy, shifts in political support
- Technological—innovations in information and other technologies, new methods in your field

What are the major opportunities or threats facing your nonprofit—related to those you serve or other stakeholders, competitors or allies, and other forces? After reviewing the information you have collected and ideas you have generated, ask the planning group to identify several opportunities and threats that seem most important in determining your nonprofit's future. Discuss if the list seems right, and then agree on those issues that will most need the planning group's attention. At this point, you might begin discussing how best to pursue each major opportunity and reduce the threats. However, most planning groups prefer to wait until Step 3 (Set Direction) to determine the best way to address these issues.

An example showing how N.E.A.R. completed Worksheet 6, Opportunities and Threats, is on the facing page.

Get Agreement on Critical Issues for the Future

A final task in taking stock of your organization is to summarize the critical issues or choices that your nonprofit faces concerning its future. In summarizing these issues you will draw upon all the other work you have just completed in Step 2—the review of your history, recent progress, mission, strengths and weaknesses, opportunities and threats, plus any other factors you think are critical. Worksheet 7, Critical Issues for the Future, on page 129 can be used to help identify these issues.

Although your organization may face many important issues or choices, we suggest you identify the four to eight issues most crucial to your nonprofit's future success. It may be helpful to state each issue in the form of a question or a goal. For example, if your organization faces a significant financial squeeze, you might state this issue in one of several ways: "How can projected deficits be avoided?" or "We need to build a financial base that can sustain our programming over the long term."

WORKSHEET 6   Opportunities and Threats

INSTRUCTIONS

1. List the major opportunities and threats that you believe your organization will face in the next two to five years that may significantly influence whether it succeeds or fails.

2. Worksheets 6a and 6b may be useful if you wish to do a more detailed analysis of your customers, competitors, or possible allies.

3. Identify the four to eight opportunities or threats that are most critical to your organization's future success.

Customers and other stakeholders	Competitors and allies	Social, cultural, economic, political, or technological forces
1) N.E.A.R. needs to be out on the street regularly – talking to business owners, seeing what their needs are, doing what we can to help them grow. 2) How much should we focus on business development beyond Rice Street? 3) There is considerable concern in the neighborhood about getting more positive activities going with young people. The new youth program could be a good first step. 4) We need to keep building good working relationships with other neighborhood groups, and find ways to involve a broader group of residents in our work (including the board).	1) It's not realistic to think that we can make significant progress on larger industrial projects by ourselves. We will need other partners like the city's Planning and Economic Development Department and Port Authority. 2) We could team up with other community development corporations across the city to work on funding and how community-based development is done.	Our biggest source of program funding for housing will likely be cut after this year. We need to find additional sources of financing.

49

Worksheet 7, below, shows the critical issues identified by N.E.A.R. at its yearly strategic planning retreat.

WORKSHEET 7   Critical Issues for the Future

INSTRUCTIONS

1. Review Worksheets 3-6. Then list critical issues or choices that your organization faces over the next two to five years.
2. Identify the four to eight most critical issues or choices.

1) How can N.E.A.R.'s business development, housing, and youth programs build on each other to improve the neighborhood?

2) Is N.E.A.R. taking on too much or too little? What's the right scale for each program?

3) We are not making as much progress as we hoped in developing or attracting larger businesses to the neighborhood. Should we change our approach?

4) Our housing strategy needs further work. How can housing efforts be more closely linked with the neighborhood's commercial vitality? Which approaches (rehabilitate existing properties, new construction, exterior improvements, increase home ownership) should receive greatest priority? Our program financing strategy also needs to be tuned.

5) The Community Building Initiative (youth program) needs similar clarity in its direction and focus.

TASK

Discuss relevant aspects of your organization's past, present, and future situation. Then identify the most critical issues or choices that the organization faces. Use Worksheets 3-7 on pages 117-129 if needed.

A Streamlined Approach to "Taking Stock"

We have described a traditional, step-by-step method of taking stock of your nonprofit's past, present, and future situation. That process—or something close to it—has been used by thousands of nonprofit organizations with good results. However, we frequently use a quicker method to take stock of a nonprofit's situation. Some organizations prefer this streamlined approach to Step 2 because it fits with their fast-moving style or they don't want to take the time for extended strategic planning. (Nonprofits that prefer the step-by-step approach to taking stock often have a very thorough, deliberate style.)

The more streamlined situation analysis is conducted in two basic steps:

- Pull together necessary background information, focusing on information that seems most relevant to your organization's situation. You can use a simple planning questionnaire like that described on page 38, Worksheets 3-7 in Section IV, or other methods noted on pages 37-38.

- Review this background information and identify critical issues for the future. A common format is to hold a planning retreat at which you review your nonprofit's progress over the past few years, review a summary of the background information gathered before the retreat, break people into small groups to identify critical issues for the future, and get agreement on critical issues.

Step 2 Summary

In Step 2 you have reviewed the history, present situation, and future opportunities facing your organization. You have looked both inside your organization and at the world in which you operate. You have summarized your conclusions and developed a manageable list of four to eight key issues or choices that you will need to address in your next phase of planning. You are now ready to set your organization's future direction (Step 3).

Step 3: Set Direction

In Step 2 you identified a number of issues or choices regarding your nonprofit's future. In Step 3 you will sort through these issues, reach general agreement on the best direction for your organization, and develop a first draft of your strategic plan. In that plan you will describe what your organization intends to accomplish over the next few years, as well as how you will begin to accomplish those goals. When Step 3 is done well, a shared vision or picture of the organization's future develops—one that is viable and engages people's energy and commitment.

As organizations approach Step 3, they often wonder how to determine the best focus and direction for their nonprofit. What is the best way to involve people in this discussion? How do you sort through the alternatives?

We have found four planning methods to be particularly useful in setting the future direction for nonprofit organizations:

- Critical issues approach
- Scenario approach
- Goals approach
- Alignment approach

You can pick one of these approaches to guide your discussion in Step 3 or use them in combination. You may be familiar with other planning techniques which can also be used with these methods. Each provides a somewhat different way for people to contribute their ideas about the direction for your nonprofit and to agree on the best alternative(s).

The critical issues approach, scenario approach, goals approach, and alignment approach are described below. This section also gives several tips for drafting your strategic plan and highlights a number of strategies we commonly see in strategic plans these days.

Critical Issues Approach

One way to clarify your nonprofit's future direction is the *critical issues approach*. At the end of Step 2 you identified several critical issues or choices concerning your nonprofit's future. In Step 3 the planning group puts these critical issues in a logical order, with the most fundamental or basic issues usually discussed first.

The planning group lists possible ways that the first issue might be answered or resolved, then selects the best solution. The second issue is then addressed, and so on, until all the issues have been answered. Previous decisions are sometimes revised in light of later decisions. As each critical issue is answered, the picture or vision of your organization's future becomes clearer. After addressing all issues, most organizations have a summary discussion in which they check to see that the organization's overall strategy is sound. At this point, you can write a first draft of the strategic plan.

Strengths and limitations of the critical issues approach

Strengths:

- The transition from Step 2 to Step 3 in the planning is usually quite natural with this approach.

- The critical issues approach works well when one or two main issues drive other issues, or the issues seem sequential.

- The approach also works well for organizations that are fine-tuning current strategies and methods.

Limitations:

- The approach does not work as well when the issues are highly interdependent or interconnected—when it is hard to determine where to begin the discussion.

- The critical issues approach builds a picture of the organization's future piece by piece. It may not be the best planning approach when an organization is considering several different scenarios for how to proceed.

Steps in the critical issues approach:

1. Sequence the issues.

2. Address each issue, building a clearer vision of your organization's future as each issue is answered.

3. Incorporate this vision into the first draft of your strategic plan.

Following is an example of how one nonprofit used the critical issues approach to set its future direction in Step 3.

Metro Deaf Senior Citizens

A small, year-old organization established by deaf seniors who primarily used American Sign Language decided to develop a strategic plan. The group had made very good progress in its start-up year—reaching out to other isolated seniors with severe hearing problems, organizing social events, advocating for changes at television stations and with the telephone company, and developing the skills required for these efforts. With all this new activity, group members decided that a strategic plan could help them agree on their next steps. With the assistance of a facilitator, they outlined a planning process which would take about six weeks to complete. At an initial half-day planning retreat, the seniors, the coordinator who worked for them, and the facilitator reviewed the group's accomplishments over the past year. They identified several new opportunities and challenges, then agreed on four critical issues which needed to be answered:

1) How many new people can we involve in the organization over the next two years? And how will these people be identified?

2) Which of our efforts should be emphasized in the future—outreach, training, advocacy, social activities? What are the priorities?

3) What do we expect from the coordinator over the next one to two years?

4) How will we raise the funds needed to support these efforts as they grow? How much will we need? Where will the funds come from? Who will be responsible?

At that same planning meeting, the seniors moved into Step 3 of the planning (Set Direction). They sequenced their four critical issues in the order noted above, then addressed each issue. On the first, after listing several possible ways to reach out to new people (for example, through family networks, physicians, and religious groups), the seniors decided that they could probably double the number of people regularly involved in their group over the next two years. They also identified three primary ways that they would reach out to new people. On the second, the group decided that all four functions of the organization should receive roughly equal priority in coming months. Three advocacy targets were also selected after brainstorming a longer list. Issues three and four were addressed in similar ways. At the end of the retreat, three seniors and the coordinator volunteered to develop a first draft of the organization's strategic plan, with some assistance from the facilitator.

The drafting group met to outline the plan. Then the coordinator and one senior developed a first draft, which was reviewed by the other members of the drafting group. The draft plan was reviewed with all members of the organization, several changes were made, and the organization's board approved the plan.

Scenario Approach

A second way to determine the best future direction for your nonprofit is the *scenario approach*. With this approach you develop several alternative visions or pictures of what your organization might look like in the future, select the best scenario, and determine how to make the transition from the present to your preferred future.

The scenario approach usually begins by asking all planning participants, a smaller committee, or the executive director to write several brief scenarios or verbal pictures (one paragraph to one page in length) describing what your organization might look like at some future time. Each scenario usually includes several common dimensions such as the overall goal of the organization, your role in the community, the services or products offered, key relationships, or how the organization is financed. The planning group then reviews each scenario, discusses its merits and disadvantages, and selects the scenario or combination of scenarios that looks best. That future picture of the organization and your approach for getting there (mission, major goals, and strategies) are incorporated into the first draft of your strategic plan.

Strengths and limitations of the scenario approach

Strengths:

- It can be quick.
- It stimulates big picture thinking. It helps people consider major shifts in emphasis or direction.
- It rapidly engages people.

Limitations:

- It is not particularly good for fine-tuning an organization or its strategies.
- Some groups have difficulty determining how to get from the present to the future they have envisioned.

On page 56 is an example of how Model Cities Health Center used the scenario approach in Step 3 of its planning.

> **Steps in the scenario approach:**
>
> 1. Identify major scenarios for the future.
> 2. Evaluate the scenarios.
> 3. Select the preferred scenario.
> 4. Incorporate this scenario into the first draft of your strategic plan.

Model Cities Health Center

In the early 1980s the advisory board and senior staff of a city-operated community health center were interested in spinning off from the city, believing that they could better serve their community as a free-standing nonprofit organization. The health center's leaders knew that they'd need a strategic plan which showed that independent status was in everyone's best interest. After completing a traditional situation analysis, the group began to see several alternative ways that the health center could position itself to serve the community. The group decided that the scenario approach—which described these alternative futures for the center—was the best way to think through the center's options.

At a planning retreat, as group members moved into Step 3, they were asked to consider different possibilities for the center's future. Each participant was then asked to take about ten minutes to complete the following assignment:

> Imagine that it is three years from now. You are a newspaper reporter writing a story on the center. You have looked at the center's mission, impact, services, personnel, financing, and relationships. Describe in a few phrases or a picture how the center looks— its focus, its impact, its services, its key relationships, and so on.

After making their notes, participants shared their visions for the health center's future. The consultant recorded the major components of each vision. The group noted and discussed the similarities and differences among the visions and agreed on four basic options for how the center might proceed:

- Continue as a division of the city's health department.

- Break off from the city. Become an independent community health clinic with ties to hospitals and other clinics.

- Become a community health and human service center that houses the organization and several other agencies serving the same target population.

- Become a component of a larger health care network which offers primary health care, preventive services, as well as other specialized services.

After the meeting, with the support of the advisory board and the city, the center's director talked with several other organizations to determine if there might be interest in the last two options. Each of the four options was then fleshed out. At the next planning meeting the director reviewed her findings and the four scenarios. Team members rated each scenario on several factors (fit with mission, fit with community needs, and financial feasibility). They then listed the relative advantages and disadvantages of each scenario. By the end of the meeting, the group agreed that the following seemed like the best direction for the center:

> Break off from the city. Become an independent community health center, housed in our own building. Establish a new and clearer identity. Expand our target group to include middle-income people. Also expand our service area. Improve staffing ratios. Ask two to three other organizations with complementary services (mental health, financial counseling, and perhaps day care) to have offices in the building. Develop and maintain ties with two to three hospitals and three to four community health clinics. Negotiate reimbursement from at least three health maintenance organizations.

Through a series of follow-up meetings and staff work, this scenario was developed and tested in greater detail, then incorporated into the center's strategic plan. With the plan, the advisory board and staff gained city approval for the center to become a free-standing nonprofit organization, and the center's assets were transferred to the new organization. Today, after many subsequent updates in the plan, the health center has developed beyond its original vision. It has evolved into three organizations which meet a broad range of community and family needs, which are also part of a larger network of private and public health centers, and which provide consultation to similar programs around the world.

Goals Approach

A third way to proceed with Step 3 of your strategic planning is to set several major goals or guidelines which guide the planning of your programs or divisions. Each program or division develops plans for how it will achieve or contribute to these goals. You then draft a strategic plan for the entire organization, which incorporates the program or division plans.

The *goals approach* is preferred by organizations that want several core principles, values, or strategic goals to guide the planning for all of their divisions or programs. For example, early in its strategic planning one nonprofit concluded that everything it undertook should lead to improvements in the economic and social vitality of ten targeted neighborhoods. Each major program was asked to determine how it might work with and assist residents to make such improvements. Key points from each program's plan then became part of the nonprofit's overall strategic plan.

Note that some nonprofits have difficulty using the goals approach early in Step 3 because they are not yet sure what their basic goals should be. In this situation you may prefer to begin Step 3 with the critical issues or scenario approach, then set basic goals to guide the planning at the division or program level.

Strengths and limitations of the goals approach

Strengths:

- The goals approach is a familiar, common-sense framework for many people: Set goals, develop strategies, develop implementation steps.

- It is good for shaping action around several values or themes.

- This approach often works well in shaping larger or decentralized organizations.

Limitations:

- The goals approach may not work well for smaller organizations that operate in rapidly changing environments with many opportunities.

- It does not work well with organizations that aren't clear about their goals or future emphasis.

Steps in the goals approach:

1. Set strategic goals or guidelines.

2. Develop strategies and plans to achieve goals (often done by each operating division).

3. Incorporate these goals and strategies into a first draft of your strategic plan.

Following is an example of how a theological seminary used the goals approach to reshape its institution.

A theological seminary

The new president and the board of a century-old theological seminary agreed that their institution needed a clearer strategy for equipping people for ministry. After taking stock of the seminary with its primary stakeholders—including the board, new administration, faculty, students, denomination officials, alumni, and other contributors—the president and core planning group drafted a document which laid out several principles and goals to guide all parts of the seminary in a more detailed planning process that would occur over the next three years. The document proposed four marks of excellence in theological education to which the seminary would be committed, then stated five strategic goals:

1) To inaugurate a revised educational program for excellence in ordained and lay ministries in the church and the world in the twenty-first century.

2) To achieve a stable student population of 850 high-quality students of diverse backgrounds, ages, and vocations.

3) To build a seminary community of living, learning, and worship which prepares persons who are excellent for ministry.

4) To ensure the financial strength and stability of the seminary.

5) To strengthen the bond of affection between the seminary and the ministries of the church.

The document also outlined a three-year process for reshaping the seminary around these marks of excellence and strategic goals. In addition, it noted how progress toward the goals would be monitored. The draft document (one kind of strategic plan) was reviewed with the board, administration, faculty, students, and other constituents. After several changes, the seminary's board approved the plan, which set a general direction for the seminary for the next ten years. The seminary's administration was subsequently restructured around the strategic goals, and teams were established to further develop and implement parts of the plan—for example, revising the seminary's educational programs and curriculum; modifying recruitment and admissions plans; and developing a new approach to housing, child care, and financial aid.

Alignment Approach

A fourth method to clarify your organization's future direction in Step 3 is the *alignment approach*. The idea is to get the parts of your organization working in sync—or in proper alignment—to accomplish your mission. The analogy is of having the wheels of a car rolling together in proper alignment. When the wheels are properly lined up, the car rolls smoothly. When one or more of the wheels are not heading in the same direction as the others, it takes more effort to move the car and the tires rapidly wear out.

Using this approach, organizational leaders determine how three critical dimensions of the organization can best be aligned: (1) the nonprofit's *mission*, (2) its *programming,* and (3) the *resources and support* needed to effectively operate the organization. This analysis is usually done in two steps.

First, the executive director or planning group outlines the organization's current plans using the mission/program/resources framework described below. N.E.A.R., the community development organization noted elsewhere in the workbook, described its current plans as follows:

> **Steps in the alignment approach:**
>
> 1. Outline current plans, using the mission/program/resources framework.
>
> 2. Identify what's working well and what needs adjusting in each dimension.
>
> 3. Determine how needed adjustments can be made.
>
> 4. Incorporate this revised picture of the organization into the first draft of your strategic plan.

Mission & Impact	Program Strategies	Resources & Support Needed

Improve the North End Neighborhood through economic development efforts that:
 	
- Strengthen the local economy
 	
- Improve the image of the neighborhood
 	
- Increase employment opportunities for area residents
	1. Assist small businesses:
	  - Loans
	  - Grants
	  - Technical assistance
	  - Entrepreneur development
	
	2. Promote commercial/industrial development:
	  - Attraction
	  - Development
	  - Loans
	
	3. Promote the area:
	  - Festival
	  - Marketing
	
	4. Improve area housing stock (through the North End Housing Agenda Committee):
	  - Rehab projects
	  - Rehab grants
	  - Home ownership counseling
	
	5. Promote youth employment and participation (through the Community Building Initiative)
		Board leadership and skills
		
		Staff leadership and skills
		
		Relationships and goodwill: in the neighborhood, with the city, with funders
		
		Financing for operations, and for projects
		
		Administrative systems

Second, after outlining the organization's current plans, the planning group identifies aspects of those plans (regarding mission, programs, or resources) that need adjusting, and how these adjustments can be made. Questions like the following can guide this discussion:

- *Regarding mission and impact*: Are the mission and desired impact clear? Is this the right mission for the future? If not, how should it be changed?

- *Regarding program strategies*: Is the organization playing the right role or roles in the community? Are the current program strategies effective? Are programs well implemented? If not, what changes are needed?

- *Regarding resources and support*: Does the organization have the resources and support it needs to support the mission and programs? Are these resources being mobilized in an effective manner? If not, what needs to change?

It is important to recognize what's working smoothly as well as where adjustments are needed. The planning group determines what changes will be needed in the coming months and years. This revised vision of the organization and its future is then incorporated into the first draft of your strategic plan.

In the example, N.E.A.R.'s board and staff reviewed the organization's current mission, programs, and resources using the alignment approach and decided to make several shifts in N.E.A.R.'s direction. These shifts can be seen in the box on the facing page.

Regarding mission and impact:

- N.E.A.R.'s mission statement needs to be revised to include the broader community development focus we are now pursuing. This broader focus and role seem right for the future.

Regarding program strategies:

- Commercial development: We need to vigorously pursue our current strategies of retaining businesses, filling vacancies, and completing visible commercial projects—on Rice Street, at Dale Crossroads, and across the district. We will establish a committee to recommend long-range commercial development plans and priorities for full board review before the end of the fiscal year. The following ideas will be considered in that planning: Solicit residents' and business owners' thoughts about potential projects and priorities; consider how commercial areas should be positioned; consider increasing loan limits; look at how potential projects can be screened to use staff time more productively; and market the availability of loan money. Staff will recommend production goals and staffing levels based on this plan.

- Industrial expansion: N.E.A.R. does not now have the capacity to take on major industrial redevelopment projects. The best role for N.E.A.R. at this time is to be a "squeaky wheel" to ensure that groups like the Port Authority, the Planning and Economic Development Department, and the legislature include North End sites in their cleanup and redevelopment plans. N.E.A.R.'s work to help existing industrial businesses expand should be merged with the commercial program above.

- Housing: Our work through the Neighborhood Housing Agenda Committee to improve the North End housing stock should continue, but we need a sharper strategy for the next two to three years, particularly with changes in program financing. We will ask the Neighborhood Housing Agenda Committee to update the housing plan. We will set production goals and assign staff based on that plan.

- Community Building Initiative: N.E.A.R.'s involvement in this initiative should continue, but our strategies need to be tied more closely to other N.E.A.R. goals and strategies. We will ask the Community Building Initiative Committee to address this issue.

- Other program issues: Other organizations will be encouraged to take responsibility for specific components of the Rice Street Festival.

Regarding resources and support:

- The marketing committee will consider several additional recommendations for promoting N.E.A.R. as an organization. These include ongoing North End committees, staff/board walkabouts, door-to-door visits, neighborhood cleanups, meetings with residents and business owners around the long-term commercial development plan, and better use of the community paper.

- We must bring new staff up to speed quickly through training and other methods.

- The finance committee will plan a session for board members to ensure that everyone understands the financial statements and answer any questions. Financial statements will be produced in-house later this year.

After the planning retreat, N.E.A.R.'s executive director and executive committee incorporated the above points into a draft of their strategic plan. The draft was reviewed by staff, board, and others who offered suggestions, and the final plan was then approved by the board. (For N.E.A.R.'s complete plan, see Appendix B, pages 87-101.)

Strengths and limitations of the alignment approach

Strengths:

- The alignment approach helps planning groups grasp the interrelationships among mission, programming, and resources. With some facilitation, groups with little background in strategic planning can identify and answer key strategic issues.

- It is a good planning method for organizations that need to fine-tune strategies that are basically working or to identify why their strategies may not be working.

- This approach works well for updating strategic plans.

Limitations

- The alignment approach is less helpful when organizations need to reposition themselves or consider several different scenarios for the future.

Select an Approach That Fits

The strengths and limitations of these four planning approaches—critical issues, scenario, goals, and alignment—are highlighted above. We suggest that you pick an approach (or combination of approaches) that fits with the kind of strategic choices your organization faces, is a method you feel comfortable with, and fits the time available.

Each of the four methods can be a useful way to engage board, staff, and others in developing a compelling vision of your organization's future. This vision is then described in the first draft of your strategic plan. Some organizations paint this vision very simply—through their mission statement and strategic goals for the future. Other organizations prefer to paint this picture of the future in more detail—by also adding the core values that will guide the organization and a vision statement which describes how their community (or the world) is different in three to five years as a result of their organization's efforts, and how they have caused this transformation to occur.

TASK

Decide which planning approach you will use in Step 3—scenario, critical issues, goals, alignment, or some combination. Use this approach to develop a vision of your organization's future. Based on this vision, develop a first draft of your strategic plan.

Tips for Drafting Strategic Plans

Select a person or group to do the drafting

Once the future direction of your organization is relatively clear, we suggest that a person (often the executive director) or drafting group be designated to develop a first draft of your strategic plan.

Agree on a format

Before beginning to draft a plan, it is a good idea to agree on its basic format—for example, the general length and major section headings. We suggest that at a minimum, you include several basic sections—a mission statement, major goals for the future, and strategies or objectives related to those goals. Add any additional sections you think are needed. Following are some of the sections we've seen in various plans over the years.

- *Executive summary*: A summary of your overall plan.

- *Mission and vision statement(s)*: A statement of what your organization hopes to accomplish or the reason it exists. (See page 42 for different approaches to writing mission statements.)

- *Values or guiding principles*: Concepts that guide or undergird your organization's decisions and actions.

- *History*: How your nonprofit got started, how it has developed, and what it has accomplished to date.

- *Organizational profile*: Basic facts and figures, current programs, and so on.

- *Situation analysis*: A brief summary of major strengths and weaknesses, opportunities and threats, and critical issues for the future. (Some plans include a separate section on critical issues that includes the proposed solution for each issue.)

- *Goals and strategies (or objectives)*: Strategic goals for the future, plus specific strategies or objectives related to each goal. Some planners like to divide these into program goals and supporting goals (also called management or infrastructure goals).

- *Service levels*: A summary of the levels of service planned for each of the next few years—for example, the number of people to be served, the number of training sessions to be held, the number of housing units to be developed, and so on.

- *Staffing levels*: A summary of the number and type of staff projected over the next few years. Some organizations include volunteers in this section.

- *Financial plans*: A projected operating budget showing sources of revenue and projected expenses by year. (If your organization has capital requirements, you may want to note how much you will need and where funds will come from.)

- *Success indicators*: Overall or specific indicators which will be used to judge future progress, impact, or success.

- *Other specific dimensions critical to your future*: Additional sections on competitors, governance, facilities, evaluation plans, marketing strategy, target population or markets, alliances or key relationships, administrative systems and support, and how and when the strategic plan will be monitored.

- *Implementation plan*: A section or separate document showing who has responsibility for advancing each major goal. Some organizations list major tasks (or objectives) for the next year, showing who is responsible for each, and the date by which each task will be accomplished.

- *Mini-plans*: Larger nonprofits with many subunits may include smaller strategic plans for each division or major program.

- *Appendices*: Additional material that supports your plans. Some organizations include some of the above sections in the appendices.

No one includes all of these elements in their strategic plan. To do so would make readers quite dizzy. Keep in mind the plan's intended audience, and develop a format that makes sense to you.[3] The key issues for an organization often influence the format of the plan. For example, if a major goal is to build a new building, you may want to include a separate section on facilities. When in doubt, keep the format simple. N.E.A.R.'s strategic plan in Appendix B may give you some ideas.

Some research indicates that thinner strategic plans that focus on several basic strategies are more frequently implemented than thicker plans with many sections, strategies, and layers.

Develop the first draft

One person often develops a first draft, then refines it in conversation with others. An alternative is for several people to draft sections that are combined into an overall plan by one person. Don't worry about getting the first draft perfect. Try to capture the vision, spirit, and general direction agreed on in Step 3. Then improve the plan through review sessions and subsequent drafts.

It is quite common for new critical issues to emerge as you are developing the first draft of your plan. For example, your financial strategies may not look so hot when you begin to project revenue and expenses for the next three years. If an important new issue emerges, take the time necessary to address that issue. Incorporate those results into the next draft of the plan.

Plans with more detail can be developed separately

Some organizations like to include an implementation section in their strategic plans. Others prefer to address implementation issues in a separate implementation document or in their yearly objectives, work plans, and budgets. More detailed (and separate) plans for marketing, fund-raising, or facilities are also often developed after a strategic plan has been approved.

Common Strategies

Our consultation and training with nonprofit groups across the U.S. and in other countries have given us the opportunity to review many organizations' strategic plans. Over the past few years, we have seen a variety of planning themes, strategies, and perspectives.[4] You may want to consider incorporating one or more of these into your own strategic planning.

Sharpen the organization

The emphasis here is on getting greater clarity or crispness on the basics: mission and goals, program effectiveness, accountability to constituents, maintaining a viable funding base, managing resources efficiently, and effectively promoting the organization. This is a "back-to-the-basics" approach. One increasingly used variation on this theme is to focus the strategic planning around your nonprofit's impact in the community—or the outcomes the organization achieves. With this approach, a nonprofit looks at its past and current impact in the community; gets clear about the impact it hopes to have in the future; decides what changes are needed in programming, structure, or resources in order to achieve better program results; and determines how the organization's impact and effectiveness will continue to be monitored and communicated.

Gain advantages associated with size

In some fields, nonprofit organizations either choose or are being forced (by contracting or competitive pressures) to grow larger. This is often done through aggressive expansion plans or through alliances or mergers with organizations that have complementary strengths. Through such growth, organizations hope to gain advantages such as reaching larger numbers of people, mobilizing greater resources toward large community issues, gaining operating efficiencies, developing more specialized services, gaining larger contracts, building a more diversified funding base, or increasing visibility and clout.

Find a niche

Other nonprofits work to carve out a clearer, distinctive role for themselves in the community. They become known for being particularly good at doing a specific type of work, and people think of them first when that issue or need is mentioned.

Simplify or downsize

We see two common variations of this basic strategy. The first is when organizations realize that they have taken on too many activities not directly related to their mission. In response, they decide to focus only on actions that directly fulfill their mission and drop or spin off the programs that do not fit. The second situation is when a nonprofit experiences funding cuts or a financial crunch and is forced to decide which programs and staff to keep. In this second situation, organizations often carefully consider how to best deploy the limited resources they still have. They may also consider merging or consolidating their best programs with another organization in order to ensure that valuable community services are maintained.

Focus on one or two success factors

Here, the organization endeavors to be a leader in its field around one or two factors which it believes are critical to future success. Typical factors include cost, clout, results, quality, innovation, responsiveness, ability to mobilize people, providing tailor-made solutions, or understanding and being trusted by particular groups. Organizations which pursue this strategy determine how every part of their organization supports their success in one or two of these factors.

Engage the community as an ally

Sometimes nonprofit groups realize that they have been operating with very weak ties to other parts of the community. They also realize that they cannot succeed in their mission unless they link with the resources and energies of other people and groups—residents, businesses, religious groups, neighborhood organizations, and public officials. These nonprofits often develop strategies such as forming closer working relationships with other parts of the community, finding ways for constituents to shape the nonprofit's goals and plans, and continually looking for ways to tap and build on others' resources and strengths.

Replicate

The strategy here is to build on proven approaches, not reinvent the wheel. These organizations keep informed of best practices in their field, then incorporate those approaches into their work. A related replication strategy reverses the approach: Organizations let others know of successful program approaches they've developed so that those approaches can be replicated in other locales.

Go after root causes

Some organizations choose to shift their energies toward changing the causes of problems, rather than simply focusing on the effects. This strategy may include prevention programs, organizing people to change community conditions, conducting research on root causes, advocacy, and public policy work.

Become entrepreneurial

Faced with financial pressures or a desire to find revenue to expand, some nonprofit organizations have focused on increasing earned income or undertaking profit-making ventures as a way to fulfill or extend their mission.

Become chaos pilots

One view is that fast-changing conditions make it very difficult to predict what will happen and therefore to plan in any detailed way. Organizations and leaders who hold this view often use an approach of artfully piloting their organizations through this chaotic, fast-changing world. Common themes in such plans include focusing on ultimate goals and broad visions, creating a culture that emphasizes getting things done whatever the circumstance, hiring people that can thrive in such an environment, giving people the flexibility and support needed to succeed, and providing enough structure and information to keep efforts moving in intended directions.

Become chaos pilots

Plan the mix of programs and funding

Some larger, more diversified nonprofits give considerable attention in their planning to the maturity and mix of their programming. By "maturity" we mean: Does a program use a new and somewhat untested approach, an approach that is rapidly being accepted, a well-tested and commonly accepted approach, or an approach that is past its prime? Does the organization have the right mix of programming in order to stay fresh and keep accomplishing its mission over time? A similar mind-set can be used to look at the mix of funding sources across programs, to examine how dependent the organization is on particular sources, and to determine what changes in the organization's funding base may be needed.

Pay attention to your organization's stage of development

A number of authors have suggested that nonprofit organizations go through predictable developmental stages—for example, a founding stage, a growth stage, and an institutional stage—and that certain challenges and issues can be anticipated at each stage.[5] In their strategic planning, some nonprofits devote time to examining their stage of development, as well as predictable developmental issues that will likely need attention.

Note sweeping trends

Some nonprofits are in industries or fields where large and powerful forces are working for or against them. (For example, health care is being affected by massive changes in delivery systems and approaches.) In such situations an organization's strategy may be to ride the crest of a new wave, insulate itself from these changes, or keep pressing to change the situation. Or when faced with many adverse forces, a nonprofit might decide that continued struggle is unwise; it may decide to end a program or shift its work to a setting where there is a better chance of success.

Balance "exploration" and "getting it done"

Researchers who have studied innovation note that there are often two different styles or stages of operating when an organization takes on something new.[6] The first is called "exploration." This is like approaching a forest for the first time and seeing a mountain peak on the other side which you wish to reach. You send out scouts to find the best way to get there. Some scouts get chased up trees by bears, some find paths which could be productive, some get lost, and one finds that there is not just one mountain but three. In this exploration stage, you depend a lot on faith, intuition, and what you (and others) have learned from past experience. At some point after getting the lay of the land, you start making commitments to the paths you will pursue and develop. Then another style of operating begins—"getting it done." You commit yourself to particular paths and courses of action, you implement, you refine. The distinction between these two stages may be useful if your organization is taking on new ventures in uncharted territory.

Make relationships central

Visitors to the U.S. sometimes comment that our organizations become so focused on tasks and transactions that the people served or the people working for the organization do not appear to be very valued. Recognizing this problem, an increasing number of nonprofits are placing more emphasis on becoming "rightly related" with the people they hope to benefit, with staff and board members, with other organizations, and with their larger community.

Rekindle the fire

The nonprofit sector has been criticized by some as having become too content, too professionalized, too greedy, too distracted, or too tired, resulting in a loss of passion, heart, and fire. A strong theme in the planning of some nonprofit groups is to make whatever changes are necessary to pursue their mission with commitment and passion.

The bibliography on pages 105-108 notes a number of books and articles that can give you further information on these planning perspectives. The above information is included in this workbook to give you a glimpse of strategies or themes that some organizations are considering in their strategic planning. Note that several of these strategies or perspectives may conflict. Don't let them confuse you. As organizations walk through the steps of the strategic planning process, their key issues usually become very clear, and good strategies to address those issues also become clear.

Step 3 Summary

In Step 3 you selected an approach to set your nonprofit's future direction. Using this approach, you clarified your organization's future mission and focus, goals, and general strategy. You then incorporated these into the first draft of your strategic plan.

In Step 4 you will refine your plan through reviews and any additional feasibility work that is needed. Then you will adopt the plan.

Step 4: Refine and Adopt the Plan

Your major tasks in Step 4 are to refine and adopt your strategic plan.

Refine the Plan

On pages 29-32 we suggested that you consider people or groups whom you would like to comment on your strategic plan before it is approved. In Step 4 you solicit these comments and make needed improvements in your plan. Through this process, you will fine-tune a first draft that was mostly on target into a plan that is right on the mark.

Many organizations review the drafts of their strategic plans with only key staff and the board. Other nonprofits prefer a much broader review process—getting comments and suggestions from many stakeholder groups. If you have not decided who should review the plan and how it will be reviewed, do so now.

Whether you review the plan with only your board and staff or with a number of constituent groups, we suggest that you give people adequate time to review it. Then ask for their frank comments. An agenda that often works well in review meetings is:

- Overview of the plan.
- What is your general reaction to the plan? Is it in the ballpark?
- What specifically do you like about each section of the plan and what problems, soft spots, or omissions do you see?
- What specific suggestions do you have about how the plan can be strengthened or improved?
- Next steps to complete the plan.

When your plan is near its final form, you may also want to ask:

- Where is there risk in this plan?
- Should our organization proceed with this level of risk or should we do something to reduce the risk?

The result of your reviews should be a plan that is both sound and doable—a plan that people understand and are committed to implementing. Remember that you will never have a perfect plan. Your organization will change continually, as will conditions in the world around you. As you act on your plan, you will get new information which may require adjustments in your vision of the future or in your plan for getting there.

> Review your plans with appropriate people and groups. Then make needed revisions.

TASK

Adopt the Plan

We recommend that your strategic plan be reviewed and approved by appropriate decision makers in the organization. In most nonprofit organizations, the board of directors reviews and approves the strategic plan. Some organizations also have key staff or other groups formally indicate their support of the plan before it goes to the board. After the plan is approved, you might also think about some way to recognize and celebrate the hard work of the people who contributed to the planning.

> Get approval of your strategic plan as needed. Then adopt the plan—and celebrate!

TASK

Step 4 Summary

In Step 4 you have refined or improved your plan through reviews with appropriate people. You have adopted the plan. In Step 5 you will begin to implement the plan and update it as needed.

Step 5: Implement the Plan

A common misconception is: "When your strategic plan is adopted, the planning is complete." A better perspective is: "When your plan is adopted, the next phase of strategic planning has begun." In Step 5 of strategic planning, you implement the plans developed in Steps 1-4, monitor progress, make midcourse corrections, and periodically update the plan. Good strategic plans need good implementation.

Implement the Plan

Part of strategic planning is assigning responsibility and setting timelines for carrying out each major goal, strategy, or task in the plan. These responsibilities and timelines are customarily noted in the strategic plan or in an accompanying implementation plan. Responsibilities are assigned to particular people, departments, programs, or task forces. After the plan is approved, these people or groups proceed with implementing their parts of the plan. The executive director or a designated group often provides general oversight to ensure that initial implementation efforts are proceeding smoothly.

Here are six tips which may help in implementing your strategic plan.

1. Good work in Steps 1-4 of strategic planning will help greatly in implementing your plan.

When we train people to do strategic planning, we are often asked, "How do you avoid the problem of an organization developing a strategic plan, then not implementing it?" Our most frequent answer is, "We typically do not see that problem. Good work in each step of planning (getting organized, taking stock, setting direction, and refining and adopting the plan) makes implementing the plan much easier." Two follow-up studies showed that the vast majority of organizations we assisted with planning met the majority of their goals a year later and were already updating their plans.

With effective strategic planning, the people responsible for implementing the plan have contributed their ideas and counsel throughout the planning process. The organization now has a compelling vision of the future—one that makes sense to people. Staff and departments have a pretty clear idea how they will move their piece of the organization in the intended direction. In fact, a number of these changes may have begun to be made by the time the plan is adopted. Implementing the plan, then, is largely a matter of continued focus on the results to be achieved, plus hard work.

2. Translate your strategic plan into yearly work plans and budgets.

Make sure that the goals, strategies, and key steps in your strategic plan are translated into objectives, work plans, and budgets for the coming year. It helps if everyone can see his or her role and responsibility. Make sure that adequate resources are budgeted to implement new goals and directions. Also make sure that your program, financial, and other reporting systems can give you the information needed to monitor progress toward the goals you have set. For example, if you plan to increase your services to a segment of the community by 30 percent, do you have a way to monitor your progress in this area?

3. Keep focused on the big goals and stay at it.

Good implementers remain guided by the major goals or results they ultimately hope to achieve. With time and experience, they get smarter about what works and what does not. Original plans are often enhanced by new opportunities and what emerges. Such people and organizations keep working toward ultimate goals, and their hard work usually results in many benefits for their communities.

4. Attend to changes and transitions.

As an organization shifts or modifies its direction, there are customarily a number of changes that affect people and programs. For example, jobs may need to change, and new skills are often required. An existing program may need to adapt or be discontinued in order to accomplish new goals. Some sensitivity and common sense in dealing with these changes are required to effectively implement a strategic plan. Organizational leaders and supervisors need to remember ways that they can help staff with such changes—through keeping folks well informed of what's planned, involving the people affected in determining how a change might best occur, reminding people of the vision for the future, and giving folks some time and encouragement to say good-bye to the old and embrace the new. Keeping a sense of momentum—for example, by using the plan as an orienting point in discussions or noting progress—can also be important in making a major organizational change.

5. Let others know your plans.

Consider who else should know about your strategic plans. Key stakeholders who know your organization's future course can be important allies in implementing the plan.

6. Periodically monitor progress.

We often suggest that an organization set one or more points to monitor progress on its strategic plan. This could be yearly, quarterly, or every six months. Following are several points which could be covered in such a review:

- Progress in meeting the overall or yearly goals in the plan. What has most contributed to or hindered our progress? What are we learning?

- Do the vision, goals, and particular strategies still seem sound? If not, what adjustments should we make?

TASK

Implement your strategic plan, periodically monitor progress, and make adjustments as needed.

Update the Plan

Most organizations update their strategic plans yearly, before they plan and budget for the coming year. Other organizations prefer to do a major update of their plan every three to five years, making minor adjustments in strategies as needed. A common method for yearly updates of the plan is:

- Reassess opportunities and threats, strengths and weaknesses, and critical issues using a planning questionnaire, worksheets, or other methods described in Step 2.

- Use one or more of the approaches noted in Step 3 to discuss whether the organization's basic strategies still make sense. What adjustments are needed?

- Revise the plan. Include any new service, staffing, and financial projections, and new implementation steps.

- Review the revised plan with board, staff, and any other appropriate stakeholders. Get approval of major changes.

- Translate the revised strategic plan into the coming year's objectives, budgets, and priorities.

TASK

Decide the interval at which your strategic plan should be updated, and revise the plan at that time or when needed.

Section II Summary

Using the steps outlined in this workbook, you have developed a shared vision of what you want your organization to accomplish over the next few years, and outlined the best path to begin to move in that direction. As you implement your strategic plan and learn more about what works and what does not, you will adjust your path and plan.

Remember that strategic planning is not an end in itself. It's a tool to enlist people's thoughts and energies in shaping your organization's future. If done well, such planning builds people's commitment to the future envisioned. It can also significantly improve your nonprofit's performance and impact. We hope that the people and communities you serve will be the ultimate beneficiaries of your planning.

Section III

Appendices
and References

Planning with Multiple Organizations and Communities

This strategic planning workbook focuses on how a nonprofit organization can plan for its future. These same basic planning steps can be adapted to aid multiple organizations, coalitions, and communities with their planning. Following are tips for planning in such settings, along with a description of five additional approaches we and others have found useful in planning with multiple groups.

When Planning with Several Organizations or a Community Makes Sense

Sometimes nonprofit organizations need to team up with other groups (other nonprofits, community groups, government, business, resourceful individuals) in order to accomplish a broad goal—for example, to increase employment for area residents, to reduce crime across a particular neighborhood, to enhance after-school activities for youth, or to advocate for a change in public policy. Or an entire neighborhood or city may wish to develop clear plans for its future. This kind of planning usually involves many people and groups who have a stake in the goals and issues being discussed.

You Can Use the Same Basic Planning Steps

When undertaking multi-organization or community-wide planning, you can use the same five basic planning steps described in this workbook: Get Organized, Take Stock, Set Direction, Refine and Adopt the Plan, and Implement the Plan.

Such planning often begins when several people or groups find that they have a common hope or concern or the desire for coordinated action. As they begin to discuss what do next, it is roughly equivalent to the beginning of Step 1 of the planning described in this workbook—Get Organized. This core group usually comes to some agreement about what it wants to do (for example, address an issue or develop a plan for joint action) and who should be involved.

Next (similar to Steps 2 and 3—Take Stock and Set Direction), a wider group usually discusses the issues and situation, then agrees on some goals and ways that the goals will be achieved. At each step of the planning, the participating groups are usually kept informed of what's going on and their ideas sought. At some point (similar to Step 4—Refine and Adopt the Plan), the proposed plans are reviewed with participating groups, their suggestions are solicited, and the plan is refined and approved by appropriate bodies. Finally, action is taken, results evaluated, and further adjustments are made (similar to Step 5—Implement the Plan).

We often see several basic differences, however, in planning with multiple organizations and communities versus planning with a single organization:

- Planning with multiple organizations and communities usually engages people and groups with a wider array of interests, concerns, and resources. In order to have a vital joint effort, you need to ensure that those varied interests and resources are well represented, heard, and actively engaged.

- The scope of such planning is often broad and complex. Attention needs to be paid to how the parts will fit together, the roles of participating groups, and how decisions will be made.

- It often takes longer to agree on the issues and goals, and to develop a shared vision for what can occur. As with individual organizations, perfect agreement is not needed (or possible) on goals and plans, but you need enough agreement and commitment to keep things moving toward shared goals. During implementation, many collaboratives set formal times (at least yearly) to review progress and to update their vision and goals.

- When planning with multiple organizations or communities, you do not customarily have the same connectedness and control as with a single organization. Therefore, maintaining a sense of momentum, progress, and success is usually critical to keeping different groups moving together.

- Over the course of the planning and implementation, new organizations or leaders may get involved and others may leave. When this occurs, new people or groups need to get "caught up" and their ideas sought; and responsibilities may need to be adjusted when a participating group leaves.

Pay Attention to Who Should Be Involved at Each Step

Pay close attention to who needs to be involved (or "at the table") in each planning step. We usually suggest that the planning/steering group lay out a proposed process for how the joint planning will proceed. At each step note what people and groups should be involved and how they will be involved. Periodically ask, "Does anyone else need to be here in order for this joint effort to succeed?" Check with participants (for example, every other meeting) to see if the planning seems on track to them. Make adjustments in the planning process, as needed, based on these check-ins.

Maintain Momentum and Celebrate Successes

As noted above, a continuing sense of momentum and progress is often critical to keeping multiple organizations or groups working together productively. Good meetings, a process that engages people's talents and energy, a compelling vision, small successes at each step, celebrating those successes, and old-fashioned encouragement all help. Strong relationships and past successes will also help you get through the rough spots.

Our books on collaboration—*Collaboration Handbook* and *Collaboration: What Makes It Work*—offer many suggestions on how to successfully undertake joint efforts with other organizations. (See the back page of this book for ordering information.)

Five Methods for Planning with Multiple Organizations and Communities

A "resident-driven" approach

One common method of community planning is to organize around deeply felt hopes or concerns among residents and others who have a stake in the issue or area. Such planning often begins with one-to-one or small group conversations about hopes and concerns that are on people's hearts and minds. As common issues emerge, both the planning and subsequent action are organized around these issues. Sometimes a threatening or tragic event motivates groups of people to action.

An example of this resident-driven approach is a neighborhood where one-to-one, small group, and broader conversations among neighbors highlighted two pressing concerns: trash being dumped in vacant lots, and a lack of lighting which residents felt contributed to crime at night. A neighborhood coalition formed and organized two task groups, which worked with city officials and others to clean up the vacant lots and improve street lighting. Next, the neighborhood coalition felt ready to take on several larger concerns, such as creating more good affordable housing, developing new employment and economic vitality in the neighborhood, and improving the parks and green space in the community. Over time, the neighborhood coalition continued to grow and made significant progress on these broader issues.

A "formal-leadership" approach

Another common method of multi-organization or community planning is for people in formal leadership positions to develop a joint plan around one or more shared goals or concerns. Often a planning group composed of representatives from those organizations meets to explore the issues, set goals, and determine how coordinated action can be taken. Planning group members keep their organizations informed at each step and get necessary guidance when needed. The planning group may also seek ideas from people outside their organizations who are affected by the decisions or who can provide needed information or resources. Once drafted, joint plans are customarily reviewed and approved by the participating organizations.

An example of this approach occurred in a medium-size city that planned to develop a huge shopping and entertainment complex. The new complex would likely change economic patterns, the highway system, and even the mind-set of the city. Spurred by this and other reasons, the mayor, city council, and other civic leaders agreed that the city needed a strategic plan. All major governmental units, business groups, and other civic entities appointed representatives to a planning group charged with developing overall goals and action plans for their city for the next five years. As an early step in this process, the steering group commissioned a survey of residents and a series of public meetings to hear their hopes and concerns. Key issues for the city were identified (including the impact of the major new development), goals were set, and plans developed to achieve each major goal. The community was successful in achieving most of those goals.

A second example of leadership-driven planning has been occurring in a number of cities across North America. These cities are establishing community-wide goals for health, economic vitality, or other factors. These are often specified as benchmarks or indicators of success. (For example, "all children will have received their immunizations upon entering school" or "we will create two thousand new living-wage jobs over the next two years.") The city's leadership usually organizes improvement efforts around those goals or indicators, and progress is monitored over several years.

A combined approach

In the combined approach strong resident-driven planning is combined with strong leadership-driven methods. (The midsize city discussed in the "formal leadership" example has elements of this combined approach—by including a community survey and public meetings.)

Here is an example in which strong leadership combined with civic participation to yield good results. A national foundation invited proposals from several cities on ways that families, neighborhoods, and larger public systems could team up in nurturing children. In one of these cities, a steering group composed of representatives from government, foundations, large nonprofits, and business provided initial guidance to a city-wide initiative that planned to respond to the foundation's request for proposals. The steering group was expanded early on to include greater parent and neighborhood representation. In developing plans for how the initiative might proceed, the steering group held multiple meetings with all of the above segments of the community to understand their hopes and concerns—with particular attention to engaging large numbers of parents. Participating organizations and governmental units approved the proposal and final plan, with many also committing some funding for the joint initiative. The governance structure for the final initiative now includes a broad-based steering group which provides general policy guidance, with program and operating decisions made at the neighborhood level.

The "get-everybody-in-the-same-room" approach

This approach can be used for single organizations, multi-organization initiatives, or community planning. The basic idea is to get all the people who influence a particular issue (or organization) into the same room—a big room—at the same time to explore the issue (or organization) from many different perspectives. These meetings, which might last from one to three days and involve thirty to three hundred participants, are often called "future search conferences."[7] Representatives from all stakeholder groups within and around "the system" or issue are invited to attend. Participants are usually asked to do some preparation (such as bringing relevant information), to keep task-focused during the conference, and to manage as much of the work themselves as possible.

The search conference itself includes work in groups, presentations to the whole group, and discussions with the whole group. In the first part of the conference, people with similar backgrounds or roles break into smaller groups to examine the history and present situation of the issue or system being considered. They also describe a desired future, as well as what's likely to occur if nothing changes. In discussing how to close the gap between the desired future and the "no-change" scenario, each group identifies several suggested "areas for action." Each group then presents its results to the large group. Conference facilitators condense this information into a manageable number of action areas, which are reviewed and refined with the large group. Participants then break into small groups again—this time to develop proposed plans for each action area. Each action area plan is reviewed with the larger group. The overall plan which results includes major tasks and responsibilities for each action area. Sometimes conference participants meet again in several weeks to review progress and make needed adjustments to their plans.

One metropolitan area used a future search conference to explore welfare reform. After a series of smaller organizing meetings, a wide variety of stakeholders—people currently receiving public assistance, legislators and public officials, business representatives, potential employers, nonprofits working on related issues, frontline workers, and others—were invited to a future search conference to determine how the broader community could proceed with new employment initiatives and related tasks.

The "assets" or "community-making" approach

A final strategy for community planning and renewal (similar to the resident-driven approach) has been called the "assets" or "community-making" approach. The strategy here is to strengthen connections among people and build on their resources—which leads to many small and large improvements in a community. Following are three variations of this approach.

One is to begin by identifying the assets which people can contribute to their community generally or to particular issues.[8] This can be done by door-to-door visits, in group settings, or with the aid of written material. Most people prefer face-to-face conversations because they help build connections among people. Such conversations might also focus on what people hope to see happen in their community. For example, one resident might highlight her skills in teaching, basic carpentry, working with children, coaching, and singing—and note how the vacant land across the street could become a great place for neighborhood children to play. After summarizing this information, it is shared—formally or informally—with others. People then take action around common hopes or goals, tapping the resources available to get things done.

A second way to do resource-based community planning is called "appreciative inquiry."[9] In this approach, people are encouraged to identify the things that give life or bring value to them. In one city, a group of residents decided to have conversations with people across several neighborhoods focusing on what was life-giving or valuable to them and their community. People were also asked about positive things which seemed ready to happen. After hearing this information, people met together again to envision and take action around shared hopes. Many small initiatives came out of this process, such as new after-school activities, as well as several larger initiatives, including new ways to link religious congregations with community development groups and a warehouse that distributes donated building products to neighborhood housing organizations.

A third and broader application of this basic strategy is sometimes called "community making."[10] It emphasizes several principles:

- *Build social capital*: Bring people together in purposeful activities that reveal shared values, strengthen social connections, and build trust. Hone skills such as active listening, creative conflict, mediation, negotiation, political imagination, public dialog, public judgment, celebration and appreciation, evaluation and reflection, and mentoring.

- *Strengthen civic infrastructure*: Actively engage "mediating institutions" such as religious congregations, social clubs, and service groups in improving the community. Increase citizen participation, civic education, volunteerism, and philanthropy. Improve government and intercommunity cooperation.

- *Mobilize community assets*: As described above.

- *Collaborate*: Effectively combine community strengths to achieve shared goals.

- *Act based on vision*: Out of greater civic connection, increased civic skill, and shared values will come many ideas and effective action to improve a community.

This strategy has been used as the basis of a number of comprehensive community improvement initiatives with good results.

The techniques and tips described throughout this workbook—for getting organized, taking stock, setting direction, refining and adopting plans, and implementing those plans—can be used in guiding the broader planning approaches described above.

N.E.A.R.'s Strategic Plan

NORTH END AREA REVITALIZATION PLANS FOR 1996 THROUGH 1999

MISSION

N.E.A.R.'s mission is to improve the North End neighborhood through community and economic development efforts that strengthen the local economy, improve the image of the neighborhood, increase employment opportunities for area residents, and build the capacity within the neighborhood for broad-based community renewal.

HISTORY AND FUTURE PLANS

N.E.A.R. was formed in 1984 to revitalize the ailing Rice Street commercial district. Over the past thirteen years N.E.A.R. has made progress toward achieving its goals by successfully completing small business improvement projects, key commercial real estate development projects, industrial equipment loans, and housing improvement projects. Most recently, N.E.A.R. has added a youth building initiative to involve "at-risk" teens in N.E.A.R.'s activities for the first time. N.E.A.R. has participated in community-building efforts by sponsoring community celebrations, initiating a joint-marketing effort among area merchants, participating in broader community-building initiatives, and facilitating discussions that address critical issues facing the neighborhood.

A note on program abbreviations in this document: CBI = Community Building Initiative; HIP = Housing Improvement Program; LISC = Local Initiatives Support Corporation; NDC = Neighborhood Development Corporation; N.E.A.R. = North End Area Revitalization; NHAC = Neighborhood Housing Agenda Committee; NPP = Neighborhood Partnership Program; UIB = Urban Initiative Board; STAR = City of St. Paul half-cent sales tax; NEC = North End Center

Successes include the completion of over two hundred commercial rehabilitation, expansion, and attraction projects that have resulted in the reduction of commercial vacancy rates on Rice Street from 40 percent in 1984 to under 10 percent currently. In addition, N.E.A.R. has developed a 15,000-square-foot mini-mall and redeveloped blighted vacant properties for productive use. These efforts have created over one hundred jobs in the process. Through the efforts of its Neighborhood Housing Agenda Committee (NHAC), N.E.A.R. has completed twenty home improvement projects and has rehabilitated its first vacant house for home ownership opportunities.

Over the next three years N.E.A.R. will continue its efforts to revitalize North End business districts by strengthening and retaining businesses, filling vacancies, completing key visible commercial real estate projects, and continuing its small business development programs. N.E.A.R. is working to develop a broader base of services to business owners while at the same time broadening N.E.A.R.'s base of fee income. By strengthening N.E.A.R.'s capacity to assist industrial businesses through providing loan funds and in formulating expansion projects, we will continue to increase job creation in the neighborhood that will provide living wage opportunities for area residents.

N.E.A.R. will continue to improve the neighborhood housing stock through implementation of the housing action plan developed by the Neighborhood Housing Agenda Committee. N.E.A.R. will assist residential property owners with visible improvement projects and rehabilitate vacant houses, creating affordable home ownership opportunities in the neighborhood. N.E.A.R. will also investigate the possibilities of new home construction.

N.E.A.R. will strengthen its collaborations and build the social infrastructure of the neighborhood by initiating the first year of a youth development program through its involvement in the Community Building Initiative (CBI) program. This program involves area youth in the planning and implementing of N.E.A.R.-sponsored activities and will include work skills development and beautification projects. N.E.A.R. will focus on collaboration and building stronger relationships with key local organizations and constituencies in all of its initiatives.

GOALS AND STRATEGIES

N.E.A.R. will pursue the following goals and strategies over the next three years.

Program Goals and Strategies:

1. Continue the commercial revitalization of Rice Street while increasing activity on other commercial streets in the North End.

- Pursue development of high-impact projects to attract viable businesses.
- Implement the Dale Crossroads and Urban Initiative programs.
- Update the targeted properties list every six months and focus on redeveloping these properties.
- More effectively market available programs/resources to area businesses.
- Work with the Port Authority and the Planning and Economic Development Department to redevelop contaminated industrial sites.
- Link local residents with jobs created.
- Develop a long-range commercial development strategy, with input from residents and area businesses.

2. Purchase, rehabilitate, and market vacant houses to create home ownership opportunities for area residents.

- Access additional sources of program funds.
- Support collaborative home ownership counseling through HOMELink.
- Pursue new construction opportunities for vacant lots.

3. Create opportunities for youth to be involved in planning and implementing community improvement projects.

- Clarify goals, roles, and responsibilities for Community Building Initiative program implementation.
- Develop community "master plan" for public spaces in the North End and undertake beautification efforts in line with that plan.
- Sponsor youth forums that address current issues and events.

4. Work to enhance the neighborhood's image and build a sense of community.

- Provide leadership in marketing the assets of the North End community.

- Sponsor community events to encourage active participation.

- Facilitate discussions that address critical issues facing the neighborhood.

- Involve more residents in N.E.A.R.'s efforts.

- Increase regular communication through presentations and articles about community concerns, successes, and plans with an emphasis on how N.E.A.R. works to address the issues.

- Strengthen N.E.A.R.'s working relationship with the District 6 Planning Council, the North End Business Club, and other key organizations to accomplish mutual goals that enhance the livability and marketability of the area.

- Identify ways in which N.E.A.R. can continue and expand its leadership role within the community.

Supporting Goals and Strategies:

5. Strengthen N.E.A.R.'s financial base.

- Implement year two of N.E.A.R.'s fund-raising plan for operating and program support.

- Increase fee income.

- Explore alternative funding to increase revenue beyond foundation, government, and corporate sources.

- Strengthen board and staff's working relationships with prospective funders.

- Install new accounting software/system.

6. Strengthen board and staff development.

- Implement board and staff training plan.

- Clarify board committee roles and relationships between staff and board committee.

- Review and update personnel policies and benefits program.

PROGRAM PRODUCTION

Projects or People Served

Business Assistance	1996-97	1997-98	1998-99
Technical Assistance (businesses)	35	35	35
NDC Micro-entrepreneur Training	16	16	18
Dale Crossroads (businesses)	0	10	10
NPP 4 Fixed Asset Loan	2	5	5
NPP 2 Facade Imp. Loan	3	4	6
NPP 16/17 Industrial Loan	2	3	3
Revolving Loan UIB	0	2	3
Foundation Loan/Grant	3	3	4
NPP 13 Grant	15	0	0
Total	**76**	**78**	**84**

Housing Program	1996-97	1997-98	1998-99
Housing Improvement Program	17	0	0
Revolving Loan Program	0	15	20
Vacant House Rehabilitation	2	2	2
Home Ownership Training	25	30	35
New Home Construction	2	2	3
Total	**46**	**49**	**60**

Community Building Initiative	1996-97	1997-98	1998-99
Part-time Employment Opportunities	20-30	20-30	20-30
Visible Improvement Projects	1/yr	2/yr	2/yr
Quarterly Youth Service Projects	4/yr	4/yr	4/yr
Sponsor Youth Forums	4/yr	4/yr	4/yr
Total	**39**	**40**	**40**

STAFFING PLAN

Full-time Equivalents

	1996-97	1997-98	1998-99
Executive Director	1.00	1.00	1.00
Small Business Development Staff	1.00	1.00	2.00
Office Manager	1.00	1.00	1.00
Housing Program Manager	1.00	1.00	1.00
CBI Program Manager	1.00	1.00	1.00
Administrative Support Staff	0.50	1.00	1.00
Total	**5.50**	**6.00**	**7.00**

FINANCIAL PLANS

Operating Budget:

Revenue	(base year) 1995-96	1996-97	1997-98
Local Business Contributions	$15,000	$15,000	$17,000
St. Paul Companies	70,000	35,000	30,000
LISC Operating Support	41,200	42,500	48,000
LISC Management Assistance Grant	5,900	7,000	6,000
Other Corporations and Foundations	35,000	87,500	103,000
NPP Administrative Grants	7,500	7,500	7,500
NHAC Administrative Grants	13,000	5,000	0
Revolving Loan Fund Admin. Fees	5,000	5,000	5,000
Fee Income	6,000	8,000	10,000
Interest on Investments	1,000	1,000	2,000
NEC Management Fee	4,200	6,000	6,000
Miscellaneous Revenues	0	0	0
Total Revenue	**$203,800**	**$219,500**	**$234,500**

Expenses			
Salaries	$120,000	$131,220	$137,500
Total Staff Benefits	12,000	11,250	11,925
Staff Recognition	500	500	600
Staff Training	3,050	8,000	8,000
FICA Taxes (Employer's Share)	9,180	10,038	10,519
State Unemployment Taxes	400	400	400
Worker's Compensation Insurance	800	800	906
Developers Service Corporation	1,250	1,500	1,750
Audit	5,000	3,000	4,000
Accounting	3,500	2,500	2,500
Professional Services	5,000	7,000	11,000
Office Expense	7,200	7,200	7,200
Office Supplies	2,300	2,700	3,000
Printing and Paper	1,500	1,700	2,000
Subscriptions and Memberships	1,200	1,200	1,200
Corporate Promotion/Advertising	3,420	3,500	4,000
Telephone Service	3,000	4,000	4,000
Postage and Shipping	1,600	1,200	1,300
Bank Charges	700	700	700
Photography	500	300	500
Mileage Reimbursement	1,200	1,000	1,000
Equipment Purchases	4,000	3,792	4,000
Equipment Repair and Maintenance	1,500	1,500	1,500
Business Insurance	3,500	3,000	3,500
Forums and Community Events	2,500	2,500	2,500
Contingency	9,000	9,000	9,000
Total Expenses	**$203,800**	**$219,500**	**$234,500**

Project Budgets:

A budget, including sources of revenue, will be developed for each major development/redevelopment project before the project begins and will be revised, if needed, with necessary approvals.

A note to readers: As part of its strategic planning, N.E.A.R. also develops an implementation plan for each of its program areas. That plan follows.

1996 IMPLEMENTATION PLANS

SMALL BUSINESS DEVELOPMENT

Program Plans:

N.E.A.R.'s Small Business Development Program provides assistance to area commercial and industrial businesses with expansions and ongoing business improvement needs. N.E.A.R. assists businesses in undertaking projects that will improve the visibility and/or viability of their operations.

N.E.A.R. maintains five revolving loan funds that provide low-interest subordinated loans and small grants for facade improvements and loans for fixed asset purchases. N.E.A.R. staff provide assistance in reviewing project plans, identifying financing sources, procuring contractor bids, and fulfilling documentation requirements.

In 1996 N.E.A.R. will add two new loan pools to the current pool of available resources. These new funds will increase the flexibility of funds available (including working capital and acquisition funds) to traditionally underserved entrepreneurs, and, for the first time, loan funds will be made available throughout N.E.A.R.'s entire service area.

N.E.A.R.'s Small Business Development Program additionally targets commercial and industrial real estate development of underutilized properties in the North End. Activities range from attracting businesses to vacant store fronts and properties to the development of parking projects and retail centers.

N.E.A.R. may act as coordinator, codeveloper, or developer in an effort to stimulate new activity on the street. N.E.A.R.'s involvement may include the following: working with local businesses to plan for development, securing financing for projects, and marketing to attract businesses to local projects. N.E.A.R. also assists in cutting "red tape" by assisting businesses with site plan reviews, zoning changes, and contractor selection. N.E.A.R. will provide maximum assistance if the assistance will contribute to the positive development of businesses in the North End area.

Staffing Plan:

The program requires a full-time small business development program manager, 10 percent of the executive director's time for supervision, and approximately 10 percent of the office manager's time. As the program expands production, additional staffing through volunteers or consultants may be needed.

Program Funding:

This program requires approximately $68,000 in funding annually. Funds to cover the overhead are generated through loan fund administration fees, loan origination fees, and general overhead fund-raising. Over the years, N.E.A.R. has received funds to capitalize the loan funds from private and public sources. Five loan funds are well established which include over $300,000 in total capital. N.E.A.R. has recently added two loan pools to its portfolio, Urban Initiative Challenge Grant Funds and City of St. Paul Half-Cent Sales Tax Funds, that bring more than $160,000 to N.E.A.R.'s program base.

Program Production:	Projects or People Served		
	1996-97	1997-98	1998-99
Technical Assistance (businesses)	35	35	35
NDC Micro-entrepreneur Training	16	16	18
Dale Crossroads (businesses)	0	10	10
NPP 4 Fixed Asset Loan	2	5	5
NPP 2 Facade Imp. Loan	3	4	6
NPP 16/17 Industrial Loan	2	3	3
Revolving Loan UIB	0	2	3
Foundation Loan/Grant	3	3	4
NPP 13 Grant	15	0	0
Total	**76**	**78**	**84**

Key Tasks in 1996:	**Responsible**	**By When**
Maintain relationships with area businesses and address needs as they arise.	John/Kris/Board	Ongoing
Implement Dale Crossroads (STAR program).	John	May 1996
Implement Urban Initiative Program.	John	May 1996
Form a steering committee to develop strategic plan for the redevelopment of key vacant sites.	John	May 1996
Assist businesses in locating in the North End.	John	Ongoing
Provide financial assistance to twenty businesses in N.E.A.R.'s service area.	John	Ongoing
Provide technical assistance to cut red tape and minimize risk and costs associated with development.	John	Ongoing
Compile and maintain an accurate inventory of all business properties in the North End.	John	Ongoing
Broaden base of services and fee income.	John/Kris/Board	Ongoing
Increase role of sponsorship of entrepreneurial training programs.	John/Kris/Board	Ongoing
Assist in leasing vacant storefronts to maintain low vacancy rates.	Staff	Ongoing
Address need for environmental cleanup.	Staff	Ongoing
Assist Port Authority and Planning and Economic Development in the redevelopment of large industrial sites.	Staff	Ongoing

NEIGHBORHOOD HOUSING ACTION PROGRAM

Program Plans:

This program was developed by the Neighborhood Housing Agenda Committee (NHAC) a joint committee of residents and business people to address the decline of the housing stock in the North End. During an eighteen-month planning process, a housing action plan was written that emphasized the need to upgrade the neighborhood housing stock, rehabilitate vacant houses, and encourage home ownership opportunities within the neighborhood.

Four strategies have been developed to achieve these goals:

- Housing Improvement Program (HIP)—Through HIP, N.E.A.R. provides matching grants to property owners to undertake visible improvement projects. The program manager works with applicants to develop a scope of work that defines the project, reviews the contractor bids for projects, monitors construction, and disburses the grant funds.

- Vacant House Rehabilitation Program—N.E.A.R. purchases vacant houses using city and private financing and rehabilitates properties for sale to create affordable home ownership opportunities.

- Home Ownership Training—In collaboration with HOMELink, N.E.A.R. offers home ownership training to prospective home buyers.

- New Home Construction.

Staffing Plan:

This program requires a full-time housing program manager, 10 percent of the executive director's time for supervision, and approximately 10 percent of the office manager's time. As the program expands production, additional staffing through volunteers or part-time administrative assistance may be needed.

Program Funding:

Funding for HIP has been provided by the City of St. Paul. Additional funds are being requested from the STAR program, local banks, and the McKnight Foundation to continue this effort. Funding for the Vacant House Rehabilitation Program comes from two sources: LISC Home Ownership Production Program and the City of St. Paul Houses to Homes Program. N.E.A.R. also receives a recoverable grant from LISC for predevelopment costs. Operating support is generated by fees from development projects and grants from corporations and foundations.

Program Production:

	Projects or People Served		
	1996-97	**1997-98**	**1998-99**
Housing Improvement Program	17	0	0
Revolving Loan Program	0	15	20
Vacant House Rehabilitation	2	2	2
Home Ownership Training	25	30	35
New Home Construction	2	2	3
Total	**46**	**49**	**60**

Key Tasks in 1996-97:	**Responsible**	**By When**
Complete 17 HIP projects.	Mike	November 1996
Acquire and rehabilitate two vacant houses for home ownership opportunities.	Mike	January 1997
Sponsor a neighborhood housing fair.	Mike	April 1997
Establish housing revolving loan program to provide low interest loan funds to projects.	Mike	May 1997
Complete planning for new construction to fill in vacant spaces.	Mike	June 1997
Identify additional sources of funding.	Kris/Mike	Ongoing
Assist HOMELink in providing home ownership training in the North End.	Mike	Ongoing
Assess current programs and develop new initiatives to respond effectively to neighborhood needs.	Mike	Ongoing

COMMUNITY BUILDING INITIATIVE (CBI) YOUTH DEVELOPMENT PROGRAM

Program Plans:

N.E.A.R. has initiated its CBI youth development program to tie its physical development strategies with the broader community. It serves to augment N.E.A.R.'s current programs while increasing involvement of youth and residents in its development activities. Through N.E.A.R.'s relationship with other area service providers we hope to augment activities of the North End Family Center by addressing an age group underserved in the community.

Staffing Plan:

This effort requires a full-time program manager, 15 percent of the executive director's time for supervision, and approximately 10 percent of the office manager's time. As the program takes shape, the services of consultants may be needed.

Program Funding:

Funding for the Community Building Initiative program has been provided for by LISC. As the program evolves, additional sources of funding may need to be generated through outside support.

Program Production:	Projects or People Served		
	1996-97	1997-98	1998-99
Part-time Employment Opportunities	20-30	20-30	20-30
Visible Improvement Projects	1/yr	2/yr	2/yr
Quarterly Youth Service Projects	4/yr	4/yr	4/yr
Sponsor Youth Forums	4/yr	4/yr	4/yr
Total	**39**	**40**	**40**

Key Tasks in 1996:	**Responsible**	**By When**
Select project to involve youth/gain momentum and public awareness of program.	Pam/Committee	January 1996
Recruit youth through committee members.	Pam/Committee	January 1996
Submit articles to local newspaper to advertise availability of program.	Pam/Committee	January 1996
Implement first project.	Pam/Committee	January-April 1996
Select first forum topic and begin collaboration with other organizations.	Pam/Committee	February 1996
Select second forum topic.	Pam/Committee	March 1996
Hold first youth forum and event.	Pam/Committee	April 1996
Select summer projects and solicit financial support.	Pam/Committee	April 1996
Sponsor first community service project.	Pam/Committee	April 1996
Celebration for first project.	Pam/Committee	May 1996
Recruit appropriate summer project supervisor.	Pam/Committee	May 1996
Advertise availability of summer program.	Pam/Committee	May 1996
Select youth summer workers.	Pam/Committee	May 1996
Hold second forum/training.	Pam/Committee	May 1996
Implement first projects working with youth.	Pam/Committee	June-August 1996
Implement youth project tied to Rice Street Festival including youth training.	Pam/Committee	July 1996
Organize community celebration to mark completion of summer projects.	Pam/Committee	August 1996
Evaluate impact of program and initiate master planning to guide program for the next two years.	Pam/Committee	September 1996
Work with area groups to develop activities for youth on a year-round basis.	Pam	Ongoing

PROMOTION OF N.E.A.R., RICE STREET, AND THE NORTH END

Program Plans:

This program involves N.E.A.R.'s ongoing sponsorship of events and activities which enhance the image of the neighborhood and build a sense of community. N.E.A.R. sponsors the Rice Street Festival Sidewalk Extravaganza and is involved in the North End Holiday Party planning. N.E.A.R. is also involved in the installation and maintenance of holiday decorations, crime prevention activities, and other efforts that improve the neighborhood. During 1994 N.E.A.R., in collaboration with the North End Business Club, implemented a commercial marketing strategy that focused on identifying Rice Street's strengths and creating a logo for commercial strip marketing efforts. The activity produced the first-ever joint-marketing effort among area merchants.

N.E.A.R. is expanding its role to include the facilitation of community-wide forums on special issues and topics of concern for community members in today's changing environment.

Staffing Plan:

This program requires 15 percent of N.E.A.R.'s executive director's time, 25 percent of the office manager's time, and 5 percent of each program manager's time to fulfill the promotion and outreach goals.

Program Funding:

Approximately $20,000 annually is needed to cover the overhead of N.E.A.R.'s community promotion efforts. Funds are allocated through our general operating support. N.E.A.R. also raises funds locally to sponsor the events associated with the program.

Key Tasks in 1996:	Responsible	By When
Sponsor the Sidewalk Extravaganza and expand/improve the event.	Board/Staff	Annually
Assist area organizations in planning the neighborhood holiday party to promote the area.	Kris/Staff	Ongoing
Notify businesses of policy changes and plans that impact their businesses.	Kris/Staff	Ongoing

SUPPORTING GOALS AND STRATEGIES

Key Tasks in 1996:	Responsible	By When
Develop training policy and schedule for staff and board.	Kris	May 1996
Approach local businesses for support.	Kris	June 1996
Increase community-planning component of N.E.A.R. through CBI Committee.	Kris/Board	June-Sept. 1996
Strengthen N.E.A.R.'s funding base and financial stability.	Kris/Campaign	August 1996
Complete implementation of the Comprehensive Fund-raising Plan.	Kris/Campaign	August 1996
Increase N.E.A.R.'s visibility/credibility.	Staff	Ongoing
Continue to implement N.E.A.R.'s marketing plan.	Kris	Ongoing
Strengthen working relationships with key organizations.	Staff/Board	Ongoing
Strengthen board and staff effectiveness.	Kris	Ongoing
Continue to work with board structure to effectively manage N.E.A.R.	Executive Committee	Ongoing

Endnotes

page 42

1. See Richard Broholm ("The Power and Purpose of Vision in Exemplary Organizations"), John Bryson *(Strategic Planning for Public and Non-profit Organizations: A Guide to Strengthening and Sustaining Organizational Achievement),* John Carver *(Boards That Make a Difference),* Peter Senge *(The Fifth Discipline: The Art and Practice of the Learning Organization),* and Support Centers of America ("What Are the Basic Steps in a Strategic Planning Process?" "What's in a Mission Statement?" and "What's in a Vision Statement?") for useful discussions of vision, mission, and values statements. Note that various authors use different terms to describe these concepts. What's important is that you develop a framework for describing your organization's purpose that makes sense to *you*.

2. Excerpted with permission from the 1994 Annual Report of the International Youth Foundation, 67 West Michigan Avenue, Suite 608, Battle Creek, Michigan 49017.

page 64

3. See Support Centers of America ("What Should a Strategic Plan Include?") for other tips. This and other helpful documents are available through their Internet site at http://www.supportcenter.org/sf/spgenie.html.

page 65

4. We thank Robert Leaver of Organizational Futures for his monograph, "The Future of Nonprofit Organizations" (1985), which stimulated our thinking about common strategies that nonprofit organizations use.

page 68

5. See Ichak Adizes (*Corporate Lifecycles: How and Why Corporations Grow and Die and What to Do About It*), Larry Greiner ("Evolution and Revolution as Organizations Grow," *Harvard Business Review*), and Karl Mathiasen (*Board Passages: Three Key Stages in a Nonprofit Board's Life*) for more on the developmental phases and challenges of organizations.

6. See Yu-Ting Cheng and Andrew Van de Ven ("Learning the Innovation Journey: Order Out of Chaos?" *Organization Science*).

page 83

7. See Marvin Weisbord (*Discovering Common Ground: How Future Search Conferences Bring People Together to Achieve Breakthrough Innovation, Empowerment, Shared Vision, and Collaborative Action*).

page 84

8. See John Kretzman and John McKnight (*Building Communities from the Inside Out: A Path Toward Finding and Mobilizing a Community's Assets*) for more on this assets-based approach.

9. See David Cooperrider and Suresh Srivastva ("Appreciative Inquiry in Organizational Life" in *Research in Organizational Change and Development*, edited by William A. Pasmore and Richard W. Woodman) and James Ludema, Mike Mantel, and Bud Ipema ("Rebuilding Cities Through Transboundary Collaboration: Lessons from Vision Chicago," 1995). Other material on appreciative inquiry is available through the Department of Organizational Behavior, Weatherhead School of Management, Case Western Reserve University, Cleveland, Ohio 44106.

page 85

10. See Allan D. Wallis ("Toward a Paradigm of Community-Making," *National Civic Review*).

Bibliography

Adizes, Ichak. *Corporate Lifecycles: How and Why Corporations Grow and Die and What to Do About It.* Englewood Cliffs, N.J.: Prentice-Hall, 1988.

Allio, Robert J., and Malcolm W. Pennington, eds. *Corporate Planning: Techniques and Applications.* New York: AMACOM, 1979.

*Allison, Mike, and Jude Kay. *Strategic Planning for AIDS Service Organizations.* San Francisco: Support Centers of America, 1994.

Andrews, Kenneth R. *The Concept of Corporate Strategy.* rev. ed. Homewood, Ill.: Irwin, 1987.

*Broholm, Richard R. "The Power and Purpose of Vision in Exemplary Organizations." Boston: Unpublished paper, 1989.

*Bryson, John M. *Strategic Planning for Public and Nonprofit Organizations: A Guide to Strengthening and Sustaining Organizational Achievement.* 2d ed. San Francisco: Jossey-Bass, 1995.

*Bryson, John M., and Farnum K. Alston. *Creating and Implementing Your Strategic Plan: A Workbook for Public and Nonprofit Organizations.* San Francisco: Jossey-Bass, 1995.

*Carver, John. *Boards That Make a Difference.* San Francisco: Jossey-Bass, 1990.

Cheng, Yu-Ting, and Andrew H. Van de Ven. "Learning the Innovation Journey: Order Out of Chaos?" *Organization Science,* 7 (Nov/Dec 1996): 593-614.

Indicates materials geared specifically to nonprofit organizations.

Cooperrider, David L., and Suresh Srivastva. "Appreciative Inquiry in Organizational Life." In *Research in Organizational Change and Development,* William A. Pasmore and Richard W. Woodman, eds. Greenwich, Conn.: JAI Press, 1987. (Other material on appreciative inquiry is available through Case Western Reserve University Department of Organizational Behavior.)

*The Drucker Foundation for Nonprofit Management. *The Drucker Foundation Self-Assessment Tool for Nonprofit Organizations.* San Francisco: Jossey-Bass, 1993.

*Egan, Anne Hayes. "Supporting Mission & Budget." rev. ed. Santa Fe: New Ventures, 1995.

*Epsy, Siri N. *Handbook of Strategic Planning for Nonprofit Organizations.* New York: Praeger, 1986.

Greiner, Larry E. "Evolution and Revolution as Organizations Grow." *Harvard Business Review*, 50 (July/Aug 1972):37-46.

*Gross, Susan. "The Power of Purpose," 1985, "The Planning Dreads: Why Groups Resist Planning," 1987; "Too Little Money or Too Little Planning?" 1987. Washington, D.C.: Management Assistance Group.

Hamel, Gary, and C.K. Prahalad. *Competing for the Future.* Boston: Harvard Business School Press, 1994.

*Hardy, James M. *Managing for Impact in Nonprofit Organizations: Corporate Planning Techniques and Applications.* Erwin, Tenn.: Essex Press, 1984.

*Kibbe, Barbara, and Fred Setterberg for The David and Lucile Packard Foundation. *Succeeding with Consultants: Self-Assessment for the Changing Nonprofit.* New York: The Foundation Center, 1992.

*Knauft, E. B., Renee A. Berger, and Sandra T. Gray, *Profiles of Excellence: Achieving Success in the Nonprofit Sector.* San Francisco: Jossey-Bass, 1991.

*Kotler, Philip, and Alan R. Andreasen. *Marketing for Nonprofit Organizations.* 5th ed. Englewood Cliffs, N.J.: Prentice-Hall, 1995.

*Kretzman, John P., and John L. McKnight. *Building Communities from the Inside Out: A Path Toward Finding and Mobilizing a Community's Assets.* Chicago: ACTA Publications, 1993.

Leaver, Robert. "The Future of Nonprofit Organizations." Providence, R.I.: Unpublished paper received in correspondence with author, 1985.

Indicates materials geared specifically to nonprofit organizations.

Lindblom, Charles E. "The Science of Muddling Through." *Public Administration Review,* 19 (1959):79-88.

Ludema, James D., Mike Mantel, and Bud Ipema. "Rebuilding Cities Through Transboundary Collaboration: Lessons from Vision Chicago," prepared for the Academy of Management Organization Dimensions of Global Change Conference, Case Western Reserve University, May 1995.

*Mathiasen, Karl, III. *Board Passages: Three Key Stages in a Nonprofit Board's Life.* Washington, D.C.: National Center for Nonprofit Boards, 1990.

*Mattessich, Paul W., and Barbara R. Monsey. *Collaboration: What Makes It Work: A Review of Research Literature on Factors Influencing Successful Collaboration.* St. Paul, Minn.: Amherst H. Wilder Foundation, 1992.

Mintzberg, Henry. "The Fall and Rise of Strategic Planning." *Harvard Business Review,* 72 (Jan/Feb 1994):107-14.

———. *The Rise and Fall of Strategic Planning.* New York: Free Press, 1994.

*Park, Dabney G., Jr. *Strategic Planning and the Nonprofit Board.* Washington, D.C.: National Center for Nonprofit Boards, 1991.

Porter, Michael E. *Competitive Advantage: Creating and Sustaining Superior Performance.* New York: Free Press, 1985.

———. *Competitive Strategy: Techniques for Analyzing Business, Industry and Competitors.* New York: Free Press, 1980.

*Safford, Dan, and PS Associates. *Strategic Planning Manual.* Seattle: United Way of King County, 1994.

*Scott, Katherine Tyler. *Trustee Education Training Manual.* Indianapolis: Trustee Leadership Development, 1991.

Senge, Peter M. *The Fifth Discipline: The Art and Practice of the Learning Organization.* New York: Doubleday, 1990.

Steiner, George A. *Strategic Planning: What Every Manager Must Know.* New York: Free Press, 1979.

*Stern, Gary J. *Marketing Workbook for Nonprofit Organizations.* St. Paul, Minn.: Amherst H. Wilder Foundation, 1990.

*Support Centers of America. "What Is Strategic Planning?" "What Are the Key Concepts and Definitions in Strategic Planning?" "What Are the Basic Steps in a Strategic Planning Process?" "What Do I Need to Know Before I Start the Planning Process?" "What Are the Individual Roles in the Planning Process?" "What's in a Mission Statement?" "What's in a Vision Statement?" "What Is a Situation Assessment?" "How Can We Do a Competitive Analysis?" "What Is a Strategy and How Do We Develop One?" "What Should a Strategic Plan Include?" "How Do You Develop an Annual Operating Plan?" "How Do We Increase Our Chance of Implementing Our Strategic Plan?" "Should I Use an External Consultant?" "How Do I Use Retreats in the Planning Process?" San Francisco: Support Centers of America, 1995. Available through Internet Web site http://www.supportcenter.org/sf/spgenie.html.

*Szabat, Kathryn, and Karen Simmons. "What Nonprofits and Grantmakers Think about Strategic Planning." Philadelphia: LaSalle University, 1995.

Treacy, Michael, and Fred Wiersema. *From the Discipline of Market Leaders.* Reading, Mass.: Addison-Wesley, Conference Presentation, ARNOVA, 1996.

*United Way of America. *What Lies Ahead: Countdown to the 21st Century.* Alexandria, Va.: United Way of America's Strategic Institute, 1989.

Wall, Stephen J., and Shannon Rye Wall. "The Evolution (Not the Death) of Strategy." *Organizational Dynamics*, 24 (Autumn 1995):6-19.

Wallis, Allan D. "Toward a Paradigm of Community-Making." *National Civic Review,* 85 (Winter 1996):34-47.

Weick, Karl. The Social Psychology of Organizing. 2d ed. Reading, Mass.: Addison-Wesley, 1979.

Weisbord, Marvin R., and thirty-five international coauthors. *Discovering Common Ground: How Future Search Conferences Bring People Together to Achieve Breakthrough Innovation, Empowerment, Shared Vision, and Collaborative Action.* San Francisco: Berrett-Koehler, 1992.

*Winer, Michael, and Karen Ray. *Collaboration Handbook: Creating, Sustaining, and Enjoying the Journey.* St. Paul, Minn.: Amherst H. Wilder Foundation, 1994.

Indicates materials geared specifically to nonprofit organizations.

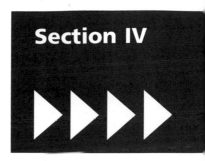

Worksheets

(Detachable for easy use and photocopying.)

INSTRUCTIONS   *(Completed example on page 25)*

1. List the benefits you expect from strategic planning as well as any concerns.
2. Note possible ways to build benefits and overcome concerns. Circle the best ideas.
3. Decide how you will proceed.

Benefits expected	Concerns	Ways to build benefits and overcome concerns

Decide how you will proceed

☐ Full steam ahead ☐ With caution, addressing the concerns above ☐ Wait until a better time to begin ☐ Stop— don't proceed

(more space on back)

Benefits expected	Concerns	Ways to build benefits and overcome concerns

(Completed example on pages 33–34)

INSTRUCTIONS

Indicate how each of the following issues will be handled. Then outline the steps, responsibilities, and timelines for developing your strategic plan.

1. You are developing a strategic plan for:
   - ☐ Your total organization
   - ☐ Total organization, plus each major program or division
   - ☐ Only part of your organization (a division or program)
   - ☐ A multi-organization initiative or coalition
   - ☐ Other:

2. For what period of time are you planning?
   - ☐ Next 2 years
   - ☐ Next 3 years
   - ☐ Next 4 years
   - ☐ Next 5 years
   - ☐ Other (specify): _____

3. What critical issues do you hope the planning will address?

4. Time devoted to planning: Which approach do you prefer?
   - ☐ "What we can do in a very limited time" approach: Under sixteen hours of planning meetings
   - ☐ A compact approach: Sixteen to thirty hours of planning meetings
   - ☐ A more extended approach: More than thirty hours of planning meetings

5. Who will manage the planning effort and keep it on track?
   - ☐ An individual:

   - ☐ A steering group: (suggested members)

   - ☐ Other:

6. Are you going to use a consultant or other resource person in developing the plan?
   - ☐ Yes   ☐ No   ☐ Unsure

   If so, what kind of help do you need?

   (Page 27 has suggestions.)

7. Note who should be involved in developing the plan. (List people or groups.)
   Note the planning steps in which they should be involved. (Check as many boxes as apply.)

	Step 1: Get Organized	Step 2: Take Stock	Step 3: Set Direction	Step 4: Refine and Adopt the Plan	Step 5: Implement the Plan
Board members					
Executive director					
Other staff or staff groups:					
Other stakeholder groups:					
Consultants and resource people:					

8. By what date do you want to have the plan approved? _____

9. Outline the steps you will use in developing your plan. After outlining the process, review it with the people involved. Finally, make any changes needed.

Steps	Responsible	By when

INSTRUCTIONS

(Completed example on page 40)

1. Review your organization's history and present situation.

2. List any historical issues or trends that will need attention as you plan for the future.

(Completed example on page 43)

INSTRUCTIONS

1. Describe below your understanding of your organization's mission or purpose.
2. List any questions, ideas, or concerns you have about your present mission.
3. Note any ideas about how your organization's mission could or should change.

Present mission or purpose

Questions about the current mission

Possible changes in the mission for the future

INSTRUCTIONS

(Completed example on page 45)

1. List the major strengths and weaknesses of your organization as it faces the future.
2. Note which strengths and weaknesses will be most critical to your organization's future success.

Strengths and assets	Weaknesses and liabilities

INSTRUCTIONS

(Completed example on page 49)

1. List the major opportunities and threats that you believe your organization will face in the next two to five years that may significantly influence whether it succeeds or fails.

2. Worksheets 6a and 6b may be useful if you wish to do a more detailed analysis of your customers, competitors, or possible allies.

3. Identify the four to eight opportunities or threats that are most critical to your organization's future success.

Customers and other stakeholders	Competitors and allies	Social, cultural, economic, political, or technological forces

(more space on back) 123

Customers and other stakeholders	Competitors and allies	Social, cultural, economic, political, or technological forces

INSTRUCTIONS

1. Note needs of current or potential "customers" or beneficiaries of your organization's services. Also note those resources you could tap or mobilize. Note ideas for how your organization might meet those needs or use those resources.

2. List other significant groups who have a stake in what you do (for example, funders, contractors, regulators, supporters). Note how you might meet their needs. Also note how you might tap or mobilize their resources.

3. Transfer major opportunities and threats to "Customers and other stakeholders" column of Worksheet 6.

Customers or beneficiaries   Describe current or possible new target groups:

Their needs	Ways to meet those needs

Their resources	Ways to mobilize or tap those resources

Other stakeholders   List group or person:

Their needs	Ways to meet those needs

Their resources	Ways to mobilize or tap those resources

INSTRUCTIONS

1. List present and possible new competitors and what you compete for. Next, note your organization's relative advantages or disadvantages (for example, quality, results, cost, ability to tailor services, other features).

2. List possible allies and how you might team up with each person, group, or organization (for example, merger, coalition, trade association, joint programming, other kinds of support).

3. Transfer major opportunities or threats to "Competitors and allies" column of Worksheet 6.

Competitors	Compete for	Your relative advantages	Your relative disadvantages
Existing			
New			

(continued) 127

Allies	How might you team up?

WORKSHEET 6b—Competitors and Allies

INSTRUCTIONS

(Completed example on page 50)

1. Review Worksheets 3-6. Then list critical issues or choices that your organization faces over the next two to five years.
2. Identify the four to eight most critical issues or choices.

Five Steps to Develop a Strategic Plan

**STEP 1
Get
Organized**

- Note why you are planning and any concerns
- Select a steering group or person to keep the planning on track
- Determine if outside help is needed
- Outline the planning process that fits your organization
- Get commitment to proceed

**STEP 2
Take Stock**
(Situation
Analysis)

- Pull together necessary background information
- Review your nonprofit's past, present, and future situation
- Identify key issues or choices

**STEP 3
Set Direction**

- Develop a vision of your organization's future
  - Critical issues approach
  - Scenario approach
  - Goals approach
  - Alignment approach
- Determine how to move the organization toward this future
- Develop a first draft of the plan

**STEP 4
Refine and
Adopt the Plan**

- Review and refine the plan
- Adopt the plan

**STEP 5
Implement
the Plan**

- Implement the plan
- Monitor progress
- Make adjustments
- Periodically update the plan

Collaboration Handbook:
Creating, Sustaining, and Enjoying the Journey

by Michael Winer & Karen Ray

Shows you how to get a collaboration going, set goals, determine everyone's roles, create an action plan, and evaluate the results. Includes a case study of one collaboration from start to finish, helpful tips on how to avoid pitfalls, and worksheets to keep everyone on track.

192 pages, softcover   *Item # AWF-94-CHC*

Collaboration: What Makes It Work, Revised

by Wilder Research Center

An in-depth review of current collaboration research. Major findings are summarized, critical conclusions are drawn, and twenty key factors influencing successful collaborations are identified. Includes the Wilder Collaboration Factors Inventory, which collaborative groups can use to assess their collaboration.

64 pages, softcover   *Item # AWF-01-CWW*

Community Building: What Makes It Work

by Wilder Research Center

Reveals twenty-eight keys to help you build community more effectively. Includes detailed descriptions of each factor, case examples of how they play out, and practical questions to assess your work.

112 pages, softcover   *Item # AWF-97-CBW*

The Wilder Nonprofit Field Guide to:
Conducting Successful Focus Groups

by Judith Sharken Simon

Shows you how to collect valuable information without a lot of money or special expertise. Using this proven technique, you'll get essential opinions and feedback to help you check out your assumptions, do better strategic planning, improve services or products, build goodwill, and more.

80 pages, softcover   *Item # AWF-99-FGC*

Consulting with Nonprofits:
A Practitioner's Guide

by Carol A. Lukas

A step-by-step, comprehensive guide for consultants. Addresses the art of consulting, how to run your business, and much more. Also includes tips and anecdotes from thirty skilled consultants.

240 pages, softcover   *Item # AWF-98-CWN*

Coping with Cutbacks: The Nonprofit Guide to Success When Times Are Tight

by Emil Angelica & Vincent Hyman

Shows you practical ways to involve business, government, and other nonprofits to solve problems together. Also includes 185 cutback strategies you can put to use right away.

128 pages, softcover   *Item # AWF-97-CWC*

The Wilder Nonprofit Field Guide to:
Crafting Effective Mission and Vision Statements

by Emil Angelica

Guides you through a six-step process that results in a mission statement, vision statement, or both. Shows how a clarified mission and vision leads to more effective leadership, decisions, fundraising, and management. Includes tips on using the process alone or with an in-depth strategic planning process, sample mission and vision statements, step-by-step instructions, and worksheets.

64 pages, softcover   *Item # AWF-01-FMV*

The Wilder Nonprofit Field Guide to:
Developing Effective Teams

by Beth Gilbertsen and Vijit Ramchandani

Helps you understand, start, and maintain a team. Provides tools and techniques for writing a mission statement, setting goals, conducting effective meetings, creating ground rules to manage team dynamics, making decisions in teams, creating project plans, and developing team spirit.

80 pages, softcover   *Item # AWF-99-FGD*

The Wilder Nonprofit Field Guide to:
Fundraising on the Internet

by Gary M. Grobman, Gary B. Grant, and Steve Roller

Your quick road map to using the internet for fundraising. Shows you how to attract new donors, troll for grants, get listed on sites that assist donors, and learn more about the art of fundraising. Includes detailed reviews of 77 web sites useful to fundraisers, including foundations, charities, prospect research sites, and sites that assist donors.

64 pages, softcover   *Item # AWF-99-FGF*

The Wilder Nonprofit Field Guide to:
Getting Started on the Internet

by Gary M. Grobman & Gary B. Grant

Learn how to use the internet for everything from finding job candidates to finding solutions to management problems. Includes a list of useful nonprofit sites, and shows you how to use the internet to uncover valuable information and help your nonprofit be more productive.

64 pages, softcover   *Item # AWF-99-FGG*

Marketing Workbook for Nonprofit Organizations
Volume I: Develop the Plan, Revised and Updated

by Gary J. Stern

Don't just wish for results—get them! Here's how to create a straightforward, usable marketing plan. Includes the six P's of Marketing, how to use them effectively, a sample marketing plan, and worksheets.

132 pages, softcover   *Item # AWF-01-MWI*

Marketing Workbook for Nonprofit Organizations
Volume II: Mobilize People for Marketing Success

by Gary J. Stern

Put together a successful promotional campaign based on the most persuasive tool of all: personal contact. Learn how to mobilize your entire organization, its staff, volunteers, and supporters in a focused, one-to-one marketing campaign.

192 pages, softcover   *Item # AWF-97-MW2*

The Nonprofit Mergers Workbook
The Leader's Guide to Considering, Negotiating, and Executing a Merger

by David La Piana

A merger can be a daunting and complex process. Save yourself time, money, and untold frustration with this highly practical guide that makes the process manageable and controllable. This unique guide includes case studies, decision trees, twenty-two worksheets, checklists, tips, milestone, and many examples. You'll find complete step-by-step guidance from seeking partners, to writing the merger agreement, dealing with typical roadblocks, implementing the merger, and more.

240 pages, softcover   *Item # AWF-00-NMW*

Resolving Conflict in Nonprofit Organizations:
The Leader's Guide to Finding Constructive Solutions

by Marion Peters Angelica

Helps you identify conflict, decide whether to intervene, uncover and deal with the true issues, and design and conduct a conflict resolution process. Includes exercises to learn and practice conflict resolution skills, guidance on handling unique conflicts such as harassment and discrimination, and when (and where) to seek outside help with litigation, arbitration, and mediation.

192 pages, softcover   *Item # AWF-99-RCN*

Five Easy Ways to Order

 Call toll-free: **1-800-274-6024**
Internationally: 651-659-6024

 Mail: Amherst H. Wilder Foundation
Publishing Center
919 Lafond Avenue
St. Paul, MN 55104

OUR GUARANTEE
If you aren't completely satisfied with any book, simply send it back within 30 days for a full refund.

 Fax: 651-642-2061

 E-mail: books@wilder.org
On-line: www.wilder.org

www.wilder.org
Want more details? Check out our web site for each book's table of contents, author information, excerpts, and quantity discounts. You can also order on-line.